Mini-Calorie Cookbook

Annette Wolter

Mini-Calorie Cookbook

Nelson

Thomas Nelson and Sons Ltd
36 Park Street London WIY
4DE
PO Box 18123 Nairobi Kenya

Thomas Nelson (Australia) Ltd
597 Little Collins Street
Melbourne 3000

Thomas Nelson and Sons
(Canada) Ltd
81 Curlew Drive Don Mills
Ontario

Thomas Nelson (Nigeria) Ltd
PO Box 336 Apapa Lagos

First published in Great Britain
in 1974

ISBN 0 17 147155 5

Printed by Smeets/Offset,
Weert, Holland.

Contents

Foreword

These photos don't lie: the dishes really do taste as they look. In one respect, however, the photos don't tell the whole story: everything illustrated is presented with the intention of helping you keep slim. And not only slim – but happy, too – for you don't have to give up good food just because you're watching your weight. The recipes are all composed in the light of the latest findings of modern nutritionists. Follow them and you'll have enough of all the nutritive substances you require to keep fit and healthy, and if you feel the need to lose weight, take a look at the section entitled 'How many calories do you need?' (page 11). Study it and you'll discover how, by staying just a little below your daily calorie ration, you can 'slim without tears'. The recipes are grouped in the traditional categories. It's up to you to decide, according to occasion or appetite, whether to omit or reduce the usual side-dishes to the main course you fancy or, instead, to compose your menu of a number of mouth-watering tit-bits. Wherever appropriate, suitable side-dishes are suggested, without necessarily the recipe being given – it's assumed you know how to cook rice, potatoes or noodles. All side-dishes are included in the tables starting on page 113, where you can ascertain exactly how many calories each represents when prepared in a certain way. Calorie-conscious cooking requires the exact measuring of all ingredients – mere estimates just won't do. You should, therefore, use always the same spoons and the same cup or glass of medium size as measuring aids. To avoid possible errors it's advisable to test the measuring instruments you normally use on your kitchen scales or a letter-balance.

There are sure to be occasions when, for some reason or other, you'll want to replace certain ingredients by others. In such cases you're strongly advised to consult the calorie table, which will tell you how generous or parsimonious you'll have to be with the planned substitution.

Enjoy your calorie-conscious cooking!

Annette Wolter

6

Becoming slim

Is there anything more reasonable than the desire to lose surplus weight? The reasons prompting this desire are not merely aesthetic — there's the fact that slim people tend to be healthier and more resistant to infection than those carrying unnecessary fat. As a German nutritionist once put it: 'Nature intended man to be slim. A fat layer of 1 cm (just over 1/3″) underneath the skin is the most human beings require as a reserve against possible nutritional deficiencies or protection against cold'.

Significantly enough, there were among his audience many slim people, who, as they listened to him, could be observed surreptitiously pinching their upper-arms and back muscles; those obviously overweight were peacefully sleeping through this — to them — boring part of the lecture.

The attitude of those of ample proportions was almost certainly due to resignation. Of course, they too would love to have been, or become, slim, but to have done so would have meant sacrificing many cherished habits which in their various ways compensate the obese for their excessive weight — the tit-bits on the bedside-table, the peanuts in front of the television screen, the beloved whisky, vodka or brandy, the ice-cream, the creamy piece of gateau or the toothsome crackling of roast pork. But enough of these transgressions against the slim line.

Compensatory nibbling of things that are fattening starts a vicious circle in that those so indulging become accustomed to excessive quantities of food, with the result that if and when they do try to change their ways, they feel quite literally 'faint with hunger'.

Of course, there are people whose excessive weight is due to psychological or organic disorders, while others may perhaps in some measure belong to a type which is naturally stocky. In all such cases it's for a doctor to determine the cause and not only to prescribe a diet but also to watch over its observance.

But let's assume you're simply one of those gluttons who habitually tend to eat just a little too much of everything tasting good and who, as a result, invariably lose the 'battle of the bulge'. It is for these people — and they're in the majority — that this book is intended, for it sets out to help you continue enjoying the pleasures of the table but with a good conscience. All you're expected to do is to go to the trouble of working out how many calories are required to keep your weight at the level it should be and act — or rather eat — accordingly, and in the course of a few weeks you'll lose an appreciable number of pounds. Provided you stick to this routine, which by then should've become a habit anyway, you'll maintain your weight at the reduced level for years and without trouble.

Becoming slim

What are calories?

Calories are units of heat, the word 'calorie' coming from the Latin 'calor' meaning heat. The term is used mainly in the field of nutrition where it means the energy required by a human being to keep his body temperature at 36.8°C (98.4°F). Energy is also required to perform such vital functions as breathing, the pumping movement of the heart and the filtering activity of the kidneys — even when asleep, a certain number of calories are required to stay alive. The minimum quantity used by the body in a state of complete rest is called the 'base metabolic rate' and varies from individual to individual, but ranges roughly between 1500 and 1700 calories.

Human beings require yet more calories to go from a state of rest to a state of movement — whether work or any other activity — and these are acquired from food. Protein, carbohydrates, fats, water, vitamins and minerals — all these body-building substances are contained in what we eat. Producing energy are proteins (1g providing 4.1 calories), carbohydrates (1g providing 4.1 calories) and fat (1g providing 9.3 calories).

Equally essential to maintaining life are the vitamins and mineral substances which, together with the proteins, carbohydrates and fat, ensure the organic functions of the body; proteins, carbohydrates and fats, as they occur in various forms of food, themselves provide some of these vital vitamins and mineral substances.

To lead a healthy and active life, therefore, you need to assimilate all the energies, nutritive substances and other active agents, contained in the various basic foodstuffs. These basic foodstuffs — cereals, fruit, vegetables, fish, meat, eggs, milk products and edible fats — contain all the essential substances the human body requires. Of course, not every basic foodstuff contains all the vital substances. Fats, meat, fish and poultry have only traces

Foodstuffs rich in Proteins

of carbohydrates or no carbohydrates at all. Many kinds of fruit are practically fat-free, while edible fats contain hardly any protein. So as you require all these substances daily, your meals should be composed of the greatest possible variety of basic foodstuffs.

Water you can forget about, for we get enough in the form of drinks, soups, fruit and all other food.

Proteins, together with water, mineral substances and vitamins have a body-building function and replace used-up substances. Without them children wouldn't grow, and adults would age prematurely. Children and people in the latter half of their life thus require a particularly rich protein diet, i.e. 1.5g (0.05oz) per kg (just over 2lb) of body weight. For example, a 12-year old boy weighing 45kg (7st 1lb)

Becoming slim

needs 67.5g of protein a day. A woman of 55 weighing 58kg (9st 1lb 10oz) requires 87g of protein daily and a 35-year old man weighing 70kg (11st) needs 70g of protein every day. Although animal proteins are more valuable to the human body than vegetable proteins, the latter are frequently particularly rich in vitamins, so your daily intake should consist of a mixture of both, such as: bread with milk or curd cheese, or pulses with meat. Buttermilk, milk, curd cheese, cheese, eggs, fish, meat and sausage contain all the more proteins the lower their fat content. Rich in vegetable proteins are porridge, rice, semolina, pulses, bread and nuts (particularly peanuts).

Carbohydrates in the form of fruit and vegetables provide — apart from energy — vitamins, mineral substances and cellulose. Cellulose, though contributing nothing that nourishes the body, acts as roughage and as such increases the bulk of our food and stimulates the digestion. Your daily intake of carbohydrates should thus consist mainly of fruit, salads and vegetables. Sugar, sweets, pasta and confectionery made from wheat flour are very rich in calories, and should be eaten

Foodstuffs rich in Carbohydrates

in moderation only. Some carbohydrates, particularly sugar, are very highly refined and have their protective materials — that is, their minerals and vitamins — removed in the refining process. Excessive use of carbohydrates is, therefore, a transgression of the rules of slimming.

Fats are the energy source richest in calories. Vegetable fats such as oils and margarine provide us with vital fatty acids, whereas animal fats, particularly butter, have a high vitamin and mineral content. All fats, provided they are taken within reason, greatly enhance the taste of our food, besides helping in the complicated chemical process by which the body assimilates certain vitamins. **Vitamins** are vital organic compounds which the human organism is unable to produce by itself. They differ from one another in that some are soluble only

Foodstuffs rich in fat

Becoming slim

in fat whereas others are soluble only in water. Vitamins soluble in fat can perform their functions in the body only if consumed together with edible fats. In most cases animal and even vegetable foodstuffs contain minimal traces of fat; even so it's a good idea to drink a glass of carrot or tomato juice with a little cream or a drop of oil. On the other hand, the juice from the frying or braising of food should be consumed as gravy or sauce as certain vitamins will have dissolved in the fat. Vitamins soluble in fat are A, D, E and K: all are sensitive to light and oxygen but relatively insensitive to heat.

Vitamins B, (Niacin) and C are soluble in water. All foods containing the vitamins in this group must as far as possible be preserved by using water (don't drown your cabbage) and, wherever possible, the vegetable liquor in the cooking process. These vitamins are sensitive to heat.

Mineral substances are necessary to enable the body to perform some vital functions. The most important substances are Calcium, Phosphorus, Sodium, Magnesium, Iron, Iodine, Cobalt, Copper, Manganese, Molybdenum, Zinc, Fluorine, Selenium, Bromine and Cadmium — provided we vary our meals we almost certainly won't run short of these. Important though vitamins and minerals are from the point of view of health and efficiency, we cannot eat them separately (unless we take them in the form of tablets) for they form an integral part of proteins, carbohydrates and fats. According to the latest findings, our food should consist of 25% protein, 40% carbohydrates and 35% fat. Modern nutritionists insist that food for human consumption should be tasty, contain much protein and not too little fat. The guiding principle should therefore be: eat well; eat food rich in protein and, possibly, in calories, but never too much!

Becoming slim

How many calories do you need?

Calorie requirements vary considerably from person to person, depending on the base metabolic rate of each individual, his constitution, and the nature of his occupation and the intensity with which he pursues it. It's difficult therefore to establish the correct calories consumption for specific bodily activities, although it's possible to approximate for certain groups of people.

Even sitting, reading or thinking use up more calories than when the body is in a state of complete rest. In cold weather additional calories are required to keep the body at its normal temperature, but as – with our heated homes and cars – we hardly ever experience cold, extra calories on this score are, nowadays, rarely needed. Things are different when it comes to bodily exertion or work, which invariably lead to the use of additional calories, though not as many as may be supposed.

For example, one hour of:

Walking	uses up 130 calories	= 100g (3½oz) ox liver (raw)
Typing	uses up 40 calories	= 1 peach
Sewing	uses up 60 calories	= 100g (3½oz) peas
Ironing	uses up 180 calories	= 100g (3½oz) lean beef
Playing tennis	uses up 340 calories	= 100g (3½oz) meat pâté
Skiing	uses up 520 calories	= 100g (3½oz) salami
Swimming	uses up 580 calories	= 100g (3½oz) milk chocolate
Gymnastics	uses up 200 calories	= 100g (3½oz) chips

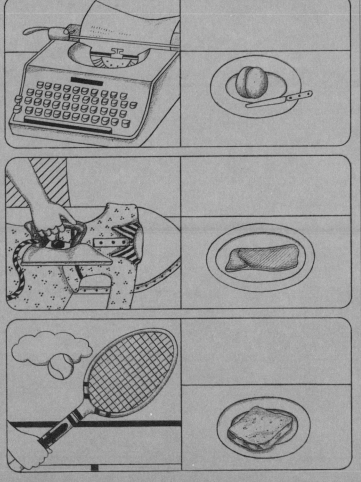

Typing
Ironing
Playing tennis

Becoming slim

You can see from these few examples how much work is necessary to be able to eat 100g (3½oz) of the things you like and stay within your daily calorie allowance. Never forget that any nourishment taken in excess of what your body requires automatically turns into fat — and any layer of fat exceeding 1cm (just over ⅓") can be harmful. A fairly accurate measure of the ideal weight of an individual can be gauged from his height.

Weights and Measures: Conversion table

1oz	= 28.368g
10g	= 0.352oz (just over ⅓oz)
1pt	= 0.567 litre (just over ½ litre)
1 litre	= 1.763pt (just over 1¾pt)
1"	= 2.539cm (just over 2½cm)
1 cm	= 0.394" (just over ⅓")

Our average daily calorie intake is a function of our ideal weight. We require per kg of body weight 32 to 34 calories daily; given a body weight of 55kg, this would be 1760 to 1870 calories for a person mainly engaged in light and predominantly sedentary work.

People performing heavy work require per kg of body weight 40 to 48 calories daily which, given again a body weight of 55kg, works out at between 2200 and 2640 calories. The above calculations are only a rough guide; as a rule of thumb, you can work out your calories in the following manner which roughly corresponds to our modern ways of life:

Allow about 3000 calories daily for adolescents up to 18 years; for men, fully-grown, following a sedentary occupation, about 2500 calories daily; for women engaged in sedentary work about 2200 calories daily and for people over 65, retired from active work, 2000 calories daily.

All this applies only to slim people who may with a good conscience say of themselves that they're maintaining their ideal weight without any fluctuations. If your scales and mirror tell you that you exceed your ideal weight considerably work out how many calories someone of your height needs and decide how many pounds you would like to lose and how quickly. If you remain about 500 to 700 calories under your maximum allowance every day, you're sure to lose weight. And even if the process takes longer than you'd hoped, don't lose patience, for fat accumulated over years is hard to shift.

Support the calorie-reducing process by as much movement in the open air as possible; walk rather than take the car — and avoid all lifts, for climbing stairs is a mighty fat reducer. Perhaps you could go swimming regularly or play tennis or go in for some other sport? Never forget that every bodily effort, every additional movement, helps you in achieving your aim.

Becoming slim

Breakfast in excess

The correct distribution of your calorie allowance throughout the day

Nutritionists have worked out various ways of distributing the allowed calories over the different meals of the day. People not suffering from weight problems but wishing to retain their ideal weight are advised to distribute the calories they require as follows: breakfast 25%, midday meal 35% and supper 25%, the remaining 15% to be allocated for such light snacks as elevenses and afternoon tea. The idea of 5 relatively small meals should be adhered to even by people wishing to slim, for it's long been proved that this division into five suits the human body best; it avoids any decline in efficiency and an overfull stomach, not to mention an excessive feeling of hunger which can so easily lead to overeating. Nutritionists specialising in slimming propose the following percentage distribution of the daily calorie allowance for people on a diet: 30% at breakfast, 10% at the morning snack, 35% at the midday meal, 10% in the course of the afternoon and 15% at supper. This works out as below:

The greatest importance is attached to breakfast because after a night's rest the body requires a fresh supply of energy-producing calories. Breakfast should be above all rich in proteins and vitamins, and this suggests — apart from wholemeal and crispbread with butter or dietary margarine — low-fat cheese, lean ham or sausage, egg, yoghurt, fruit juices or fruit. Coffee or tea may be good stimulants but the sugar should most decidedly be replaced by a dietary sweetener. A suitable mid-morning snack keeping within the recommended 120 to 180 calories may be found in the table on page 115. As for midday meals, please consult the recipes section where you'll find a great number of suggestions for low-calorie dishes.

Daily Calorie Allowance	Breakfast	Mid-morning snack	Midday meal	Afternoon snack	Supper
1200	360	120	420	120	180
1500	450	150	525	150	225
1800	540	180	630	180	270

Becoming slim

As far as the evening meal is concerned, it's important to remember that the later it's consumed the less time there is for the calories it provides to be used up prior to bed. It is, therefore, sensible to reduce your calorie intake in the evening and be content with a soup containing few calories or a slice of crispbread and fruit.

How to save calories

If you're not far from your ideal weight, eat what you like but in portions small enough to ensure that you don't exceed your calorie allowance. It's a regrettable fact, however, that those who love sweet dishes, fat gravy, pasta or sweet drinks use so much of their calorie allowance on these foods that little is left for any main course.

There's only one thing to do: exercise a little self-control and discover new delights in other fields. Oysters, lobsters, crayfish, fish with a low fat content, young poultry and above all game and wild fowl are all delicious, rich in vitamins and mineral substances, and will help you to forget your old favourites, with their excessively high calorie content and without any particular nutritive value, such as sugar, sweets in the form of pastry, gateaux, ice cream or chocolate, confectionery and pasta made from wheat flour, pulses and all dishes obviously oozing fat. Try fruit desserts sweetened with a little dietary sweetener or with a tiny quantity of honey or sugar.

Cooking entirely without fat is not to be recommended for the simple reason that fat greatly enhances the flavour of many dishes, and besides, by using fat moderately you can save many calories. Moreover, there are nowadays frying-pans and saucepans on the market lined with silicone and these, together with aluminium foil, are a great help in saving fat.

Try, when planning your meals, to give preference to protein-rich food, leaving it to wholemeal bread, fruit or vegetables to supply the carbohydrates you require. Avoid alcohol; allow yourself at most ¼ litre (½ pint) of wine per day, but don't forget to debit your calorie account with the appropriate 160—180 calories.

Another way of helping you save calories is to purchase some of the many calorie-reduced foodstuffs on sale. Among these are curd cheese and yoghurt from skimmed milk, skimmed milk powder, special jams and fruit preserves with a low calorie content, fruit juices, soups and ready-made dishes, as well as starch-reduced bread and rolls.

Enough of theory — it's time to discover for yourself what tasty dishes a calorie-conscious cook can dish up.

The Recipes

The meaning of the symbols accompanying the recipes:

Δ   The recipe is easy to follow.

Δ Δ   The recipe is not quite so easy. You should, therefore, adhere to it strictly.

Δ Δ Δ The recipe assumes your readiness to carry out somewhat more difficult or complicated operations with patience.

O   The suggested dish is not costly to make.

OO   The dish is in the medium price range.

OOO The dish is relatively expensive.

*   The cooked dish keeps fresh for four weeks, if frozen at a temperature of minus 35°C (-31°F) and stored at minus 18°C (0°F).

**   The cooked dish, if deep-frozen, will keep for up to three months, if stored at minus 18°C. (0°F).

***   The cooked dish, if deep-frozen, keeps for nine to twelve months, if stored at minus 18°C.

The recipes are intended for 4 people, whereas the calories are for a single person.

Soup is permissible

Chicken Soup with Rice
△ ○ ○

Approx. 220 calories per person

75g (3oz) rice
2½ cups water
500g (18oz) boiled chicken
    meat without bones or
    skin
¼ packet dried soup vege-
    tables (or 1 onion,
    1 carrot, 1 leek and
    1 piece of celery, all
    cleaned, washed and
    diced)
¾ litre (1½ pt) instant
    chicken stock
4 tomatoes
2 tablespoons finely
    chopped parsley

Preparation time: 25 min-
utes.

Put the rice, together with
the water, in a saucepan and
cook for 18 minutes over
mild heat. Bone chicken
and remove skin. Alterna-
tively, you can mince the
chicken. Put the soup vegetables, the chicken meat and
the instant stock into a
second saucepan and allow
to simmer over mild heat
for 5 minutes. Make some
incisions at the bottom end
of the tomatoes, scald them
and let them lie in the
water for a few minutes;
they are then ready to be
peeled, cut into eighths and
warmed up in the chicken
soup. Add the rice to the
soup, stir well and sprinkle
with parsley.

Illustration below

Suitable second course:
Tuna en Cocotte (recipe on
page 37).

Chicken Soup with Rice, recipe above

Soup is permissible

Simple Chicken Soup
△ ○ *

Approx. 120 calories per person

1 small onion
1 teaspoon butter
3/8 litre (¾ pt) milk
2 level tablespoons flour
1/8 litre (¼ pt) water
2½ tablespoons instant chicken stock
a pinch of white pepper
1 can asparagus tips

Preparation time: 15 minutes.

Peel and dice the onion. Melt the butter in a saucepan and lightly fry the diced onions in it; add the milk and bring nearly to the boil. Stir the flour into cold water, add the nearly boiling milk and bring to the boil just once. Reduce the heat, adding the instant stock to the soup and season with the pepper to taste.

Heat the asparagus tips in the soup.

Suitable second course: Chinese Prawns (recipe on page 47) or Stuffed Artichokes.

Illustration below

A tip: If you've a little cooked poultry meat left over you could add it to the soup, but you must reckon 30 calories per tablespoon of additional meat.

Simple Chicken Soup, recipe above

Soup is permissible

Herb Soup – Munich Fashion
△ ○

Approx. 85 calories per person

¾ litre (1½ pt) water
3 level teaspoons instant meat stock
a bunch of chervil (100g or 3½oz)
3 tablespoons single cream
2 level tablespoons flour
2 egg yolks

Preparation time: 20 minutes.

Bring water to the boil and dissolve instant meat stock in it. Rinse chervil, dry and chop it. Stir the cream, first with the flour and then with the egg yolks, whisk into the soup and bring to the boil once. Remove soup from the fire and mix the chervil into it. Season with a little salt and pepper to taste.

Illustration on page 17

Tomato Soup
△ ○

Approx. 45 calories per person

8 tomatoes
¾ litre (1½ pt) instant meat stock
a bunch of fresh chervil (or parsley)
1 tablespoon tomato ketchup
2 tablespoons tomato purée
2 tablespoons single cream
1 small can (150g or 5½oz) asparagus tips

Preparation time: 20 minutes.

Make a few incisions at the bottom end of the tomatoes, scald them, leave them for a few minutes in the water until they are ready to be peeled and cut into eighths. Heat up the dissolved instant meat stock, add the tomato wedges, cover and allow to simmer over low heat. Wash and finely chop the chervil. Mix the tomato ketchup and tomato purée with the cream and chervil; stir this mixture into the soup and add the asparagus tips. Now let the finished soup get thoroughly warm over very mild heat.

Suitable second course: Peasant's Delight (recipe on page 29).

Semolina Soup
△ ○ * * *

Approx. 65 calories per person

1 onion
1 tablespoon oil
3 level tablespoons coarse semolina
¾ litre (1½ pt) water
3 level teaspoons instant meat stock
2 tablespoons chopped chives
a pinch each of salt and pepper

Peel and dice onions; heat oil in saucepan and lightly fry onions in it. Slowly stir semolina into it and fry till golden brown. Gradually fill up with the water, cover and allow to thicken for 5 minutes over mild heat. Remove soup from stove to add the instant meat stock, salt, pepper and chives.

A hint: If the soup is to be deep-frozen, don't add the chives until the soup is defrosted and reheated.

Soup is permissible

Amsterdam Carrot Soup

△ ○ * *

Approx. 125 calories per person

6 carrots
¼ celeriac
1 onion
2 tablespoons butter
1 litre (almost 2 pt) instant meat stock
2 level tablespoons flour
½ teaspoon salt
¼ teaspoon pepper
a good pinch of grated nutmeg
4 tablespoons chopped parsley

Preparation time: 20 minutes.
Cooking time: 30 minutes.

Scrape and wash carrots and slice them very finely. Thickly peel celeriac, wash thoroughly and cut into small dice. Peel and dice onion. Melt butter in a saucepan and in it lightly fry the sliced carrots, diced celeriac and onion for a few minutes; then pour instant meat stock over it, cover and let cook for a further 20 minutes over low heat. Pass soup through a sieve; mash vegetables in a liquidiser and return to soup. Stir flour into a little cold water, add to the soup which should now be brought to the boil several times, while being constantly stirred. Season with salt, pepper and grated nutmeg and sprinkle the chopped parsley over it before serving.

Recommended second course: Egg Salad Paradeiso (recipe on page 39) and crispbread.

A tip: If the soup is to be deep-frozen, add parsley only when it's been defrosted for use.

Mussel Soup

△ ○ ○

Approx. 130 calories per person

200g (7oz) mussels preserved in their own juice
1 carrot
1 onion
½ leek
3/8 litre (¾ pt) water
½ teaspoon salt
2 sprigs parsley
1 tablespoon butter
1 level tablespoon flour
2 tablespoons single cream
½ cup white wine

Preparation time: 30 minutes.

Drain mussels in a sieve. Scrape, wash and coarsely grate carrot. Peel onion and cut into eighths. Cut leek lengthwise, wash thoroughly and slice thinly. Put the vegetables with the water, salt and parsley sprigs into a saucepan, cover and cook for 20 minutes over low heat. Pass the vegetable bouillon through a sieve. Melt the butter in a saucepan, stirring the flour into it and cook for a short time. Now add cream and then slowly the vegetable bouillon, bringing the lot to the boil, stirring all the while. Pour in the white wine, letting it get thoroughly hot over mild heat, but without

Soup is permissible

bringing it to the boil. The cold mussels are now distributed into 4 small soup bowls and the hot soup poured over.

Fish Soup
△ ○ *

Approx. 85 calories per person

2 onions
1 bunch soup vegetables
250g (9oz) haddock, including fins and bones
2 peppercorns
½ bay leaf
1 level teaspoon salt
1 litre (almost 2 pt) water
200g (7oz) filleted cod
2 tablespoons single cream
2 level tablespoons flour
½ teaspoon mustard
1 tablespoon tomato ketchup
¼ teaspoon white pepper
1 tablespoon capers
2 tablespoons chopped dill

Preparation time: 45 minutes.

Peel onions and cut into eighths. Clean and cut soup vegetables. Rinse the haddock and put it together with the onion eighths, soup vegetables, peppercorns, bay leaf, salt and

water in a saucepan, cover and cook over low heat for 15 minutes. Rinse cod fillets and cut into little pieces of equal size. Pass fish broth through sieve, put cod pieces into the broth and let them simmer over low heat for 10 minutes. Whisk together the cream, flour, mustard, ketchup and white pepper, adding this mixture to the soup after it has cooked for ten minutes. Now add the capers, warming the soup once again throughly. The dill is sprinkled over the soup the last minute before serving.

A tip: If the soup is enriched with 100g (3½oz) of shrimps, it will contain 30 calories more per person, but this addition turns the soup into a festive main course. If the soup is to be deep-frozen, add the dill only after it's been defrosted and is ready for use.

Recommended Dessert: Garnished Fruit Jellies (recipe on page 106).

Salsify Soup
△ ○ ○ * *

Approx. 185 calories per person

1 tablespoon vinegar
3 level tablespoons flour
2 cups water
300g (11oz) salsify
2 tablespoons butter or margarine
1 litre (almost 2 pt) vegetable broth
½ teaspoon salt
a pinch of pepper
2 tablespoons finely chopped chives
1 egg yolk
2 tablespoons single cream

Preparation time: 1 hour.

Mix the vinegar with 1 tablespoon of flour and the cups of water. Peel, wash and dice the salsify, putting them at once into the vinegar and flour. Before starting the cooking process, rinse the diced salsify once again, put them into the water, add a pinch of salt, cover and let cook for 40 minutes. Melt the butter or margarine to make a roux with the remaining flour, gradually adding the vegetable liquor. The remaining salt, pepper and chives are now added to the soup as well as the diced salsify, the lot then being heated thoroughly. Whisk the egg

Soup is permissible

yolk with the cream, adding a little of the hot soup. Take the soup off the fire and thicken with the egg yolk-cream mixture.

Illustration below

Suitable Savoury: Grilled Cheese and Tomatoes (recipe on page 37).

A hint: If the soup – which is in any event rather rich in calories – is to be served as a main dish, add a few minced meat balls (which you either buy canned or prepare yourself from minced beef), a few chopped onions and parsley, as well

as an egg and some bread-crumbs. This adds another 150 calories per person.

Spinach 'Kaltschale'
△ ○

Approx. 60 calories per person

1 egg
400g (14oz) fresh spinach
1 cup water
½ teaspoon salt
1 beaker yoghurt made from skimmed milk
a pinch each of pepper and garlic powder
about 8 ice cubes

Preparation time: 20 minutes.
Cooking time: 10 minutes.

'Kaltschale' is the German word for cold soup, made usually of fruit, but sometimes also of vegetables. Put the egg in boiling water and let it cook for 10 minutes. Pick over and wash the spinach. Bring the cup of water to the boil and steam the spinach until it is soft; place it into a flat dish and cut it coarsely. Rinse egg under cold running water, peel and dice it. Mix together the spinach with its liquor and the yoghurt, pepper and garlic powder; gently stir in the diced egg. The Spinach 'Kaltschale' is now poured into 4 soup bowls and left to cool for 10 minutes in the refrigerator. Before serving, put one to two ice cubes into each bowl.

Illustration on page 101

Suitable second courses: Asparagus and Ham Omelette (recipe on page 31) or Tuna Salad Minorca (recipe on page 24).

Salsify Soup,
recipe on facing page

23

Light Meals

Shrimps in a Piquant Sauce
△ ○ ○ ○

Approx. 235 calories per person

250g (9oz) canned or deep-frozen shrimps or prawns
4 tablespoons cream
a bunch of parsley
4 tablespoons mayonnaise
1–2 teaspoons tomato ketchup
a dash or two of Worcester sauce
2 teaspoons brandy

Preparation time: 10 minutes (deep-frozen shrimps or prawns take 3 hours to thaw).

The canned shrimps or prawns should be briefly rinsed and drained; the parsley should likewise be rinsed and then dried. The cream is whisked till semi-stiff, mixed with the mayonnaise and tomato ketchup and seasoned to taste with the Worcester sauce and the brandy. Separate the shrimps or prawns, distribute them into 4 cocktail glasses, pour the sauce over and garnish each glass with a sprig of parsley.

Illustration on facing page

Best eaten with: crackers or toast.

Tuna Salad Minorca
△ ○

Approx. 185 calories per person

1–2 oranges according to size
1 can tuna fish of 100g (3½oz)
1 tomato
1 small can anchovy fillets
1 pickled cucumber
6 stoned green olives

Preparation time: 15 minutes.

Cut from the middle of the orange 4 slices, with the peel, each about 4–5 mm (rather less than ¼″) thick. The remaining orange pieces are then squeezed. Drain the tuna fish, keeping the oil. Slice the tomato and cut off the outer rim from each slice. Add the inner part of the tomato to the tuna fish oil. Rinse and drain anchovy fillets. Cut the pickled cucumber into strips. Halve the olives. Cut the tuna fish pieces into even-sized dice and mix them with the anchovy fillets, the olive halves and the cucumber strips. Stir together the oil-and-tomato mixture and the orange juice and pour over the salad. Distribute the salad into four glasses, garnishing each with the tomato strips and stick an orange slice on the rim of each glass.

Illustration on facing page

Goes well with: crackers or toast.

Chicken Salad with Pineapple
△ ○ ○ ○

Approx. 310 calories per person

1 egg
300g (11oz) cooked chicken meat with skin and bones
150g (5½oz) canned asparagus tips
100g (3½oz) canned button mushrooms
2 slices canned pineapples
a small bunch of parsley
a few strips of canned pepper
3 tablespoons mayonnaise
2 tablespoons curd cheese from skimmed milk
1 tablespoon water
1 tablespoon pineapple juice
a pinch each of salt and pepper
a few slices of canned truffles

Preparation time: 20 minutes.

24

Shrimps in Piquant Sauce (bottom); Tuna Salad Minorca (middle); Chicken Salad with Pineapple (top); recipes on this ▷ page

Light Meals

Bring a little water to the boil and put the egg in it for ten minutes. Remove skin and bones from chicken and cut the meat into even-sized strips. Cut the pineapple slices into small pieces. Wash and drain the parsley and drain the pepper strips. Rinse the egg under cold water before peeling and dicing it. Now stir together the mayonnaise with the curd cheese, water, pineapple juice, salt and pepper; finally mix the meat strips, diced egg, asparagus tips, button mushrooms and pineapple pieces with the sauce. Distribute the salad into four bowls or glasses, garnishing each with the truffle slices, pepper strips and parsley.

Illustration on page 25

Goes well with: wholemeal bread or toast.

Olives in Aspic
△ △ ○

Approx. 120 calories per person

9 sheets white gelatine
3 eggs
1 cup deep-frozen peas
½ litre (1 pt) water
a dash of vinegar
½ teaspoon salt
*a pinch each of pepper and
    paprika*
1 cup canned mushrooms
½ cup pickled peppers
15 stuffed olives

Preparation time: 25 minutes.
Cooling time: 3 hours.

Soak the gelatine leaves in cold water. Put the eggs into boiling water and cook for 10 minutes. Cook peas in 2 tablespoons water over low heat for 6 minutes with the saucepan covered. Bring to the boil the water together with the vinegar, salt, pepper and paprika; remove from heat. Squeeze the gelatine well and stir into the hot liquor to dissolve it. Drain the mushrooms and cut into fine slices. Cut peppers into strips and the olives into thin slices. Rinse eggs under cold water before peeling and slicing them. Drain peas. Line four moulds or cups with a little of the liquid gelatine, dis-

tribute into each container a slice of egg, a few peas, the mushroom slices, pepper strips and sliced olives. Pour some more of the gelatine liquid over and allow to set for a short time. Then you repeat the process, finishing up with the remaining gelatine liquid. Put the containers into the refrigerator to set for 3 hours. To serve, dip the containers briefly into very hot water before turning the aspics onto small plates. A little parsley garnish is optional.

Illustration on facing page

Goes well with: toast and lean uncooked ham.

Olives in Aspic, recipe above ▷

Light Meals

Mixed Vegetable Salad

△ ○

Approx. 265 calories per person

1 small cauliflower
1 egg
250g (9oz) canned peas
250g (9oz) canned mush-
    rooms
280g (10oz) canned aspara-
    gus pieces
a generous pinch of pepper
2 level teaspoons sugar
½ teaspoon salt
½ teaspoon herb mustard
a dash or two of Angostura
    bitters
1 tablespoon wine vinegar
2 tablespoons mayonnaise
some parsley and tomato
    slices to taste

Preparation time: 35 minutes.

Cook the cauliflower in a
little unsalted water for
20–25 minutes, keeping the
lid on the saucepan. Put the
egg in boiling water and
cook it for ten minutes.

Drain the peas, mushrooms
and asparagus pieces. Rinse
the egg under cold water,
peel and dice it. Rinse the
cauliflower briefly before
draining and separating it
into individual heads (the
stem and the cauliflower
liquor may be used for a
soup). Stir together the pepper, sugar, salt, herb
mustard, Angostura, wine
vinegar and mayonnaise.
The finely diced egg is now
folded into the mixture. Put
all the vegetables together
into a bowl and pour the
mayonnaise dressing over it.

Mixed Vegetable Salad, recipe above

Light Meals

You may like to garnish the salad with a little parsley and slices of tomato.

Illustration on facing page

Goes well with: escalope of veal nature and boiled potatoes.

Peasant's Delight
△ ○

Approx. 175 calories per person

a bunch of chives
100g (3½oz) very lean cooked ham
400g (14oz) cottage cheese
¼ teaspoon salt
a generous pinch of coarsely ground pepper

Preparation time: 15 minutes.

Wash and dry chives and cut them finely with the kitchen scissors. Remove all fat from the ham before cutting it into strips. Mix cottage cheese with the salt, pepper and strips of ham and garnish with the chives.

Illustration below

Goes well with: crispbread, wholemeal or rye bread.

Peasant's Delight, recipe above

Light Meals

Stuffed Artichokes
△△○○

Approx. 350 calories per person

4 artichokes
1 level tablespoon salt
½ teaspoon pepper
½ teaspoon mustard
2 eggs
100g (3½oz) cooked ham
  in slices
100g (3½oz) cooked mussels
  in their natural juice
2 tomatoes
4 tablespoons cream
2 tablespoons mayonnaise

Cooking time for artichokes:
50 minutes.
Preparation time: 45 minutes.

Cook the artichokes in plenty of salted water for 50 minutes, keeping them covered. Lift them out of the water, drain them and remove the inner leaves as well as the seeds so that the firm artichoke bottom is plainly visible. Mix the vinegar with the pepper and mustard and pour the mixture on to the artichokes, leaving them to marinate for 30 minutes. Cook the eggs in boiling water for ten minutes. Cut the ham into thin strips. Drain the mussels and halve them. The tomatoes are now washed, cut in half, the pips re-

moved, and the flesh cut into strips. Pour away the marinate from the artichokes but keep it for later use. Rinse the eggs under cold water, before peeling and cutting them into eighths. Beat the cream till stiff and mix it together with the mayonnaise and artichoke marinate. Gently mix the ham strips with the cream sauce. Fill the artichoke with the mussels, tomato strips and egg wedges. Pour the sauce over it and place on top one egg wedge and a few tomato strips per artichoke.

Illustration on facing page

Goes well with: toast.

Emperor's Salad
△○○

Approx. 135 calories per person

1 egg
1 slice of calorie-reduced
  toast

1 teaspoon butter
a pinch of garlic powder
1 lettuce
a few anchovy fillets
50g (2oz) blue-vein cheese
1 tablespoon oil
1 tablespoon wine vinegar
½ teaspoon salt
¼ teaspoon pepper

Preparation time: 20 minutes.

Cook egg for ten minutes. Cut toast into small dice. Heat butter in a saucepan, fry bread dice on all sides till brown, sprinkle garlic powder over it and allow to get cold. Separate lettuce leaves, removing the imperfect ones as well as the hard stalk, tear large leaves into smaller pieces, wash several times in cold water and dry. Rinse anchovies under cold water before draining and cutting them into thin strips. Dice the cheese. Rinse the egg under cold water, peel and dice it. Stir together the oil with the wine vinegar, salt and pepper. The lettuce leaves are now gently mixed with the anchovy strips, diced egg and cheese before the dressing is poured over. Finally, sprinkle the diced bread croutons over the salad.

Illustration on page 32

30

Stuffed Artichokes, recipe above ▷

Light Meals

Italian Salad
△ ○ ○

Approx. 175 calories per person

1 small cauliflower
1 egg
6 medium-sized potatoes
150g (5½oz) deep-frozen peas
100g (3½oz) deep-frozen French beans
100g (3½oz) deep-frozen diced carrots
a bunch of radishes
some anchovy fillets
100g (3½oz) canned mushrooms
2 tablespoons oil
1 tablespoon wine vinegar
½ teaspoon salt
¼ teaspoon pepper
1 tablespoon chopped parsley

Preparation time: 40 minutes.

Wash the cauliflower and steam it in a little water, covered, for 20 minutes. Boil egg for ten minutes. Peel, wash and dice potatoes, cooking them in a little water with a pinch of salt for 15 minutes. For the last 8 minutes, add the deep-frozen peas, beans and carrots, cover them and cook them with the potatoes. Rinse the egg under cold running water, peel and slice it. Allow cauliflower to cool before separating into individual sprigs. Wash and slice radishes. Briefly rinse anchovy fillets and drain them. Now the individual cauliflower sprigs, the peas, beans, carrots, diced potatoes, anchovy fillets and the drained mushrooms are gently mixed together and put into a bowl. The oil is mixed with the vinegar, salt and pepper and poured over the salad, which is finally garnished with the parsley and the egg slices.

Illustration on facing page

Goes well with: lean cooked ham or veal escalope nature.

Asparagus and Ham Omelette
△ ○ ○

Approx. 300 calories per person

500g (18oz) fresh asparagus
¼ litre (½ pt) water
½ teaspoon salt
200g (7oz) very lean cooked ham
4 eggs
1 packet of white sauce
a wedge of processed cheese
a dash of Worcester sauce
2 tablespoons oil
2 tablespoons chopped parsley

Preparation time: 40 minutes.

Peel the asparagus, removing the woody ends; cut the asparagus into approximately 2 cm (¾") long pieces. Bring the water with the salt to the boil before adding the asparagus and cooking them over medium heat for 20 minutes. Dice the ham. Separate the eggs. Prepare the sauce according to instructions, using ¼ litre (½ pt) of the asparagus liquor, melting the cheese in it and adding the diced ham. Drain the asparagus and add it, together with the Worcester sauce, to the cheese mixture. Whisk the egg whites till stiff. Beat the egg yolks and carefully fold

Emperor's Salad (top), recipe on page 30;
◁ Italian Salad (bottom), recipe on this page

Light Meals

under the whites. Heat a little oil in a frying-pan, pour a quarter of the omelette mixture into it, cover and allow to set over low heat for about ten minutes. Repeat this three times. Place on half of each a quarter of the asparagus and ham mixture, sprinkle with parsley and fold over. The omelettes should be served immediately as they quickly lose their fluffiness. The best way to proceed is to get one omelette ready at a time and serve it before starting on the next.

Goes well with: various kinds of green salad or tomato salad.

Stuffed Tomatoes in Aspic
△ △ △ ○

Approx. 60 calories per person

¼ litre (½ pt) tomato juice from a can
2 heaped teaspoons powdered red gelatine
1 tablespoon lemon juice

1 teaspoon chopped onion
a dash of tabasco sauce
a pinch each of salt and pepper
1 egg
½ fresh cucumber
1 tablespoon oil
1 tablespoon wine vinegar
a pinch each of salt and pepper
1 tablespoon chopped mixed herbs

Preparation time: 15 minutes.
Cooling time: 3 hours
Finishing touches: 15 minutes.

Stuffed Tomatoes in Aspic, recipe above

Light Meals

Pour the tomato juice into a saucepan and warm over low heat. Soak the gelatine powder in 2 teaspoons of water and allow to soften a little. Add the lemon juice, the chopped onion, tabasco sauce, salt and pepper to the tomato juice and bring to the boil, while constantly stirring. The dissolved gelatine powder is now stirred into the tomato juice and allowed to set slightly. Rinse a ring mould with cold water before pouring the tomato aspic into it and putting it into the refrigerator for three hours. Boil the egg for 10 minutes. Separate the lettuce leaves, removing imperfect ones and hard bits and tearing the larger leaves into smaller pieces. The remaining lettuce leaves are now washed several times in cold water and dried thoroughly. Wash the cucumber and slice it unpeeled on the mandoline. Mix the oil with the vinegar, salt, sugar and finely chopped herbs. Toss the lettuce leaves and cucumber slices in the salad dressing. Rinse the egg under cold running water, peel and cut it into eighths.

To serve hold the ring mould briefly under hot water and turn the tomato aspic onto a plate. The salad is filled into the centre of the aspic and the eggs put on as garnish.

Illustration on facing page

Goes well with: lean ham or veal cutlets nature and white bread.

Substantial Cucumber Snack
△ ○ ○

Approx. 170 calories per person

2 eggs
1 fresh cucumber
140g (5oz) shrimps
½ teaspoon salt
2 tablespoons wine vinegar
3 tablespoons oil
1 tablespoon soya sauce
½ teaspoon sugar
2 tablespoons chopped dill

Preparation time: 15 minutes.

Boil the eggs for ten minutes. Peel the cucumber only if the skin is hard, otherwise wash it unpeeled and cut it into small dice of even size.

Separate the shrimps and mix them with the diced cucumber. Stir together the salt, vinegar, oil, soya sauce and sugar and gently stir this mixture into the salad. Rinse the eggs under cold water, peel them and cut them into eighths. Fill the salad into a bowl or four individual smaller bowls, sprinkling the dill over it. The egg wedges are used as garnish.

A good second course to: Semolina Soup (recipe on page 20) and best eaten with crispbread.

Stuffed Cucumber
△ ○

Approx. 105 calories per person

2 eggs
1 fresh cucumber
3 anchovy fillets
5 radishes
150g (5½oz) curd cheese
*   from skimmed milk*
½ teaspoon salt
½ teaspoon mustard
a good pinch of white pepper
1 teaspoon chopped parsley
1 teaspoon chopped dill
4 tomatoes

Light Meals

Preparation time: 25 minutes.

Boil the eggs for 10 minutes. Cut the cucumber into 8 pieces of equal size and hold these for three minutes in a sieve in boiling water. Hollow the cucumber pieces. Rinse the eggs under cold water before peeling and dicing them. Chop the anchovy fillets; wash and grate the radishes. Mix the curd cheese with the diced egg, anchovies, grated radishes, salt, mustard, pepper, parsley and dill and fill

the hollowed-out cucumber pieces with this mixture. The tomatoes are now washed and cut in half, and half a tomato is placed on each of the stuffed cucumber pieces.

Goes well with: wholemeal bread and butter.

Stuffed Apples
△ ○ ○

Approx. 195 calories per person

4 apples
4 perfect lettuce leaves
2 teaspoons lemon juice
½ cup canned mandarin
   segments
2 cups cooked and diced
   chicken meat without
   skin or bones
½ cup shredded pineapple
   from a can
150g (5½oz) curd cheese
   from skimmed milk

36   Stuffed Apples, recipe above

Light Meals

1 tablespoon each of pine-apple and mandarin juice
½ teaspoon salt
a generous pinch of white pepper

Preparation time: 30 minutes.

The apples are washed and the upper third cut off. The remaining two thirds are hollowed out and the hollowed-out fruit flesh is cut into small pieces. Then cut the rim of the apples in a zig-zag fashion, sprinkling a little lemon juice over them. Wash and dry the lettuce leaves. Drain the mandarin segments and cut them into small pieces before mixing them with the shredded pineapple. Stir together the curd cheese with the fruit juice, salt and pepper and add it, together with the apple cubes, to the other ingredients. Fill the salad into the hollowed-out apples and place them on the salad leaves.

Illustration on facing page

Goes well with: crackers or crisp bread.

Grilled Tomatoes with Cheesespread
△ ○

Approx. 120 calories per person

4 large ripe tomatoes
1 tablespoon oil
200g (7oz) cottage cheese
4 tablespoons Parmesan cheese
1 level teaspoon salt
½ teaspoon pepper

Preparation time: 15 minutes.

Wash tomatoes and cut them into 3 thick slices each. Heat oil in a frying-pan and fry the tomato slices over medium heat on one side only. Remove the slices from the pan onto a flat surface. Mix the cottage cheese with the Parmesan, salt and pepper, spread it on the uncooked side of the tomato slices; now place the tomato slices on the grill pan and grill till golden brown.

Goes well with: parsley potatoes and lean ham.

Tuna Fish and Cocotte
△ ○

Approx. 195 calories per person

200g (7oz) canned tuna fish
1 level tablespoon flour
½ teaspoon salt
¼ teaspoon pepper
1 cup water
½ cup milk
½ cup canned celeriac
300g (11oz) deep-frozen French beans

Preparation time: 15 minutes.
Cooking time: 20 minutes.

Preheat oven to 175°C (350°F; gas mark 4). Drain the tuna fish, keeping one tablespoon of the oil. Separate the fish into small pieces. Heat the oil to make a roux with the flour, salt and pepper, gradually filling up with the water and milk, stirring well until the sauce has slightly thickened. Now add the fish pieces and vegetables. Distribute the mixture into four oven-proof cocottes or scallop shells and gratinate in the oven for 20 minutes.

Goes well with: sticks of French bread or toast.

Light Meals

Bamberg Asparagus Salad
△ ○ ○

Approx. 115 calories per person

750g (27oz) fresh asparagus
1 level teaspoon salt
a pinch of sugar
1 egg
1 onion
2 tablespoons oil
1 tablespoon wine vinegar
2 tablespoons chopped pars-
ley

Preparation time: 40 minutes.

Carefully peel the asparagus, cutting off the woody ends.

Cut them into 5 cm (2″) long pieces. Bring plenty of water with the salt and sugar to the boil, put the asparagus into it and cook over medium heat for 20 minutes. Boil the egg for ten minutes, rinse under cold water, peel and cut into eighths. Drain the asparagus (keeping the asparagus liquor for a soup) and let them get cool. Peel and dice the onion, mix it with the oil, vinegar and chopped parsley, and gently stir the dressing into the asparagus pieces. Garnish the salad with the egg wedges.

Illustration below

Shrimp Salad

△ ○ ○

Approx. 180 calories per person

280g (10oz) shrimps
150g (5½oz) cottage cheese
1 tablespoon mayonnaise
1 tablespoon water
1 teaspoon mustard
1 teaspoon lemon juice
½ teaspoon salt
2 tablespoons chopped
*   parsley*
1 teaspoon capers

Preparation time: 20 minutes.

Remove the shrimps from the can and put them into a sieve for a quick rinse under cold water. Select a few of the best shrimps, and put the remaining ones together with the cottage cheese, mayonnaise, water, mustard, lemon juice and salt into a liquidizer to purée. Fill the mixture into four individual bowls or glasses and garnish with the remaining shrimps, the parsley and capers.

Goes well with: wholemeal bread or crackers.

Bamberg Asparagus Salad, recipe above

Light Meals

Egg Salad Paradeiso
△ ○

Approx. 220 calories per person

3 eggs
½ beaker yoghurt from
*   skimmed milk*
3 tablespoons curd cheese
*   from skimmed milk*
1 teaspoon lemon juice
¼ teaspoon mustard
½ teaspoon sugar
¼ teaspoon paprika
2 tablespoons chopped pars-
*   ley*
200g (7oz) sliced tongue
4 tomatoes
½ teaspoon salt

Preparation time: 15 minutes.

Boil the eggs for ten minutes. Stir together the yoghurt, curd cheese, lemon juice, mustard, sugar, paprika and parsley. Roll up the tongue slices; wash the tomatoes and cut them into eighths. Rinse the eggs under cold water, peel and cut likewise into eighths. Arrange the egg and tomato wedges, as well as the tongue rolls, in a bowl or four individual glasses and sprinkle the salt over them. The curd cheese dressing is poured over the salad just before serving.

Illustration below

Goes well with: toast or crispbread.

Egg Salad Paradeiso,
recipe above

Fish and Shellfish

Cod in Madeira Sauce
△ ○ ○

Approx. 340 calories per person

*1kg (2¼lb) cod, cut into 4
    portions*
juice of ½ lemon
1½ teaspoons salt
2 carrots
¼ celeriac
½ leek
½ parsley root
a bunch of parsley
*1 small can mushrooms
    (100g/3½oz)*
1 orange
2 pieces ginger in syrup
2 litres (4 pt) water
2 tablespoons vinegar
2 tablespoons oil
1 bay leaf
3 peppercorns
4 juniper berries
1/8 litre (¼ pt) Madeira
1/8 litre (¼ pt) white wine
a pinch of pepper
a pinch of dried basil

Preparation time: 50 minutes.

Rinse the fish slices quickly under cold running water and dry them. Sprinkle over them 2 teaspoons lemon juice and ½ teaspoon salt and let them marinate for 15 minutes. Scrape, wash and dice the carrots. Peel the celeriac thickly, wash thoroughly and cut into thin strips. Halve leek length-ways, wash under cold water and slice thinly. Rinse, dry and chop the parsley root and halve the parsley. Drain and thinly slice the mushrooms. Cut the orange into four slices and the ginger into strips. Bring the water with the vinegar and the rest of the salt to the boil, place the fish into it, reduce the heat and simmer for 15 minutes. Heat the oil in a small sauce-pan and in it lightly fry the carrots, celeriac, leek, parsley root and chopped pars-ley for two minutes, stirring continuously. Add the bay leaf, peppercorns, juniper berries, the Madeira, white wine and mushrooms, cover and cook over low heat for 15 minutes.

To serve, place the fish into a preheated dish garnishing each portion with a piece of orange and a few ginger strips. Season the sauce with the pepper and basil. Remove bay leaf. Serve sauce separately.

Illustration on facing page

Goes well with: plain boiled rice, plain boiled potatoes or French bread.

Grilled Halibut
△ △ ○ ○

Approx. 245 calories per person

*4 slices halibut, each
    weighing 150g (5½oz)*
2 teaspoons lemon juice
½ teaspoon salt
¼ teaspoon pepper
2 tablespoons oil

Preparation time: 20 minutes.

Wash and dry the halibut slices. Sprinkle them with the lemon juice. Mix the salt and the pepper with the oil and brush over the fish on both sides. Grill the halibut slices on a charcoal grill, an electric grill or in a grill-pan for five minutes on each side, brushing them over several times with the oil mixture.

Illustration below

Goes well with: potato salad or French bread and green salad.

Cod in Madeira Sauce, recipe on this page ▷

Fish and Shellfish

Baked Haddock
△ △ ○

Approx. 260 calories per person

1kg (2¼lbs) haddock
1 tablespoon lemon juice
1 level teaspoon salt
3 leeks
2 carrots
1 parsley root
¼ celeriac
¼ teaspoon pepper
4 fresh sage leaves or a
*   pinch of dried sage*

Preparation time: 30 minutes.
Cooking time: 90 minutes.

Wash the fish quickly, dry it and cut it into four thick slices. Sprinkle them with the lemon juice and salt. Soak an unglazed earthenware dish for at least 10 minutes in cold water. Remove the root-end and the bad leaves from the leeks, which are then halved lengthwise, washed thoroughly and sliced finely. Scrape the carrots, wash and cut them into thin batons.

Peel the celeriac thickly, brush thoroughly and cut into thin batons also. Remove the dish from the water and place the vegetables into it. Place the fish slices on top and spinkle with the pepper and sage. Place the dish on the bottom shelf of the cold oven and cook for 90 minutes at 250°C (450°F; gas mark 8).

Illustration below

Goes well with: parsley potatoes.

Grilled Halibut, recipe on page 40

Fish and Shellfish

Mussels in White Wine Sauce
△ △ ○ ○ ○

Approx. 200 calories per person

1/8 litre (¼ pt) water
1 teaspoon lemon juice
600g (22oz) mussels from a jar, in their own juice
1 onion
1 tablespoon butter
1 level tablespoon flour
1/8 litre (¼ pt) white wine
¼ teaspoon pepper
a pinch of sugar
2 tablespoons cream

Preparation time: 20 minutes.

Bring the water with the lemon juice to the boil. Place the mussels with the liquid from the jar into the water; lower the heat and warm the mussels for 5 minutes in the water, which should simmer but not boil. Chop the peeled onion. Strain the mussels, retaining the liquid, and keep them warm. Melt the butter, lightly fry the onions, dust over with flour and continue cooking thoroughly. Then

stir in the mussel liquor. Bring the sauce to the boil once, stirring all the time. Add the white wine, pepper, sugar and cream and heat through — without letting it boil — stirring continuously. Add the mussels to the sauce and serve at once.

Goes well with: French bread and Melon Salad (recipe on page 94).

Baked Haddock, recipe on facing page

Fish and Shellfish

Plaice Paupiettes

△ △ ○ ○

Approx. 235 calories per person

4 fillets of plaice at 90g
    (3oz) each
a little lemon juice
100g (3½oz) French beans
100g (3½oz) carrots
a pinch of salt
4 cloves
⅛ litre (¼ pt) wine
5 tablespoons single cream
1 egg yolk
a pinch each of sugar, salt,
    paprika and ginger
100g (3½oz) canned shrimps

Preparation time: 20 minutes.
Cooking time: 20 minutes.

Wash and dry the fillets of plaice, sprinkle them with lemon juice. Top and tail the beans, remove any strings and wash them. Scrape and wash the carrots and cut them into batons. Cook the beans and carrots in a small quantity of salt water for about 10 minutes. Salt the plaice fillets, divide the vegetables over them, roll up the fillets and secure them with a wooden skewer and stick one clove into each roll. Pour the white wine into a saucepan, place the paupiettes into it, cover and cook for 15 minutes over low heat. Whisk together the single cream, egg yolk, sugar, salt, paprika and ginger. Lift the paupiettes out of the white wine, stir the egg yolk mixture into the wine, bring it to the boil and reduce the heat at once. Return the paupiettes to the sauce, add the shrimps, cover and heat through without letting it come to the boil again.

Illustration on page 46

Goes well with: mashed potatoes.

Mussel Ragout 'au Gratin'

△ △ ○ ○

Approx. 250 calories per person

250g (9oz) canned mushrooms
450g (1lb) canned mussels
    (in their own juice)
4 level tablespoons flour
1 tablespoon oil
2 tablespoons butter
½ cup milk
4 tablespoons single cream
a pinch each of salt and
    pepper
2 tablespoons grated
    Emmental cheese

Cooking time: 20 minutes.

Preheat oven or grill to maximum temperature. Drain the canned mushrooms and mussels, retaining the liquor of the mussels. Turn the mussels in the flour, heat the oil in a frying-pan and briefly fry the mussels in it on all sides. Now add the mushrooms and heat them up with the mussels. Melt the butter in a saucepan, sprinkle the remaining flour into it, stir until cooked; pour in the mussel liquor and the milk.

Fish and Shellfish

Mix in the cream and season with the salt and pepper. Add the mussels and mushrooms to the sauce. Divide this mixture into four small greased fireproof dishes and bake in the oven for 10 minutes. Sprinkle over each dish some grated cheese and put into the oven or under the grill until the cheese begins to melt and brown slightly.

Illustration below

Goes well with: toasted white bread.

Fillets of Plaice in Herb Sauce
△ ○ ○

Approx. 125 calories per person

600g (22oz) frozen fillets of plaice
juice of 1 lemon
4 pieces of foil
1 teaspoon oil
½ teaspoon salt
¼ teaspoon pepper
a good pinch of garlic powder
2 tomatoes
½ leek
a bunch of parsley
a bunch of chives
1 teaspoon butter

Preparation time: 35 minutes.
Cooking time: 20 minutes.

Preheat the oven to 225°C (435°F; gas mark 7). Defrost the fillets of plaice, sprinkle them with the lemon juice and leave for 20 minutes. Brush the pieces of foil with the oil.

Mussel Ragoût, recipe opposite

Fish and Shellfish

Lay each fillet of plaice on the foil and season each with the salt, pepper and garlic powder. Securely wrap them up in the foil and bake in the oven on the middle shelf for 20 minutes. Make a crosswise incision on the rounded end of the tomato, pour a little boiling water over them and leave them for a few minutes in the water, then peel and slice them. The leek is halved lengthwise, washed thoroughly and thinly sliced. Wash and dry the herbs and chop them finely. Melt the butter in a small saucepan, lightly fry the leek, add the tomato slices and herbs and then 1—2 teaspoons water. Cover and cook for five minutes over low heat.

To serve, arrange the fillets on warmed plates and pour over the herb sauce.

Goes well with: French bread or Potato Salad (recipe on page 93).

Fillets of Plaice in Herb Sauce, recipe on page 44

Fish and Shellfish

Festive Fillets of Sole

△△○○○

Approx. 310 calories per person

*300g (11oz) deep-frozen
    lobster or crabmeat
500g (18oz) deep-frozen
    fillets of sole
juice of ½ lemon
½ teaspoon salt
¼ litre (½ pt) instant stock
100g (3½oz) canned mush-
    rooms
1 tablespoon butter
½ teaspoon flour
1/8 litre (¼ pt) white wine
1 egg yolk
4 tablespoons single cream*

Preparation time: 30 minutes.
Cooking time: 30 minutes.

Defrost the lobster or crab-
meat, keeping covered.
Sprinkle the lemon juice
over the defrosted sole fillets, season with the salt,
cover and let marinate for
20 minutes. Preheat the
oven to 100°C (225°F; gas
mark 1). The fillets of sole
are put into a saucepan with
the lemon juice; the dis-
solved instant stock is
poured over and allowed to
simmer over low heat for
15 minutes. The cooked
fillets are then arranged on a
preheated serving dish and
kept warm in the oven. Now
drain and thinly slice the
mushrooms. Heat the butter
in a pan, stir in the flour
and cook it. Work in the
cooking liquor from the fish
fillets and bring to the boil,
stirring continuously. Add
the prawns and mushrooms
to the sauce and stir over
low heat to warm through.
Now stir in the wine and
heat without letting it boil.
Whisk together the egg yolk
and cream, mix in a little of
the hot sauce and then stir
this mixture into the sauce,
take off the heat at once
and pour over the fillets.

Goes well with: plain boiled
rice or Potato Salad (recipe
on page 93).

Chinese Prawns

△○○○

Approx. 255 calories per person

*600g (22oz) deep-frozen
    prawns
½ leek
4 tablespoons oil
½ cup deep-frozen peas
½ teaspoon cayenne pepper
1 level teaspoon celery salt
½ teaspoon ground ginger
1 level teaspoon sugar*

Preparation time: 20 minutes.

Defrost the prawns (which
takes about three hours),
rinse them under cold water
and dry. Remove any bad
leaves from the leek, cut it
in half lengthwise, wash
thoroughly and slice very
thinly. Heat the oil and fry
the prawns in it until uni-
formly light brown. Add the
peas and leek, cover and
cook over low heat for 6
minutes. Season with the
cayenne pepper, celery salt,
ginger and sugar.

Illustration on page 48

Goes well with: plain boiled
rice or French bread.

Fish and Shellfish

Savoury Fish Paupiettes

△△○○○

Approx. 225 calories per person

*4 fillets of haddock weighing
    150g (5½oz) each
1 tablespoon lemon juice
1 level teaspoon salt
a bunch of dill
4 tablespoons tomato purée
¼ litre (½ pt) hot water
4 tablespoons single cream
1 egg yolk
½ tablespoon paprika
1 teaspoon butter*

Preparation time: 10 minutes.
Cooking time: 15 minutes.

Wash the fish fillets quickly under running cold water and dry them. Cut each fillet in half lengthwise, sprinkle with the lemon juice and salt. Wash, dry and chop the dill and spread with the tomato purée over the fillets. Roll the fillets up, securing them with wooden toothpicks. Stand the fillets side by side in a shallow pan, pour the hot water around them, cover and cook over low heat for 15 minutes. Whisk together the cream, egg yolk and paprika and stir in a little of the hot cooking liquor. Add this mixture to the fish paupiettes and remove at once from the heat. Melt the butter in the sauce, stirring it lightly and serve.

Goes well with: toasted white bread and green salad.

Scampi in Herb Sauce

Approx. 315 calories per person

*2 tablespoons hot water
4 tablespoons butter
600g (22oz) frozen scampi
½ onion
2 egg yolks
1 teaspoon lemon juice
¼ teaspoon pepper
¼ teaspoon salt
2 tablespoons chopped
    fresh dill
a pinch each of chervil and
    tarragon*

Preparation time: 30 minutes.

Melt 1 tablespoon butter in the hot water in a saucepan. Add the scampi to the hot liquid, cover and warm over low heat for 10 minutes.

Chinese Prawns, recipe on page 47

Fish and Shellfish

Peel and finely chop onion and cook for a few minutes in the white wine. Take the pan off the heat and stir in the egg yolks one after the other. Put the pan into a waterbath – just boiling – heat it through and, stirring continuously, add the rest of the melted butter, drop by drop. Finally stir in the lemon juice, again drop by drop, adding the pepper, salt, dill, chervil and tarragon. Pour the sauce over the scampi and mix the whole well together. Don't let the sauce boil again. Serve at once.

Goes well with: French bread or plain boiled rice and Savoury Chicory Salad (recipe on page 91)

Vegetable and Fish Ragoût
△ ○

Approx. 210 calories per person

800g (28oz) haddock with-
    out skin and bones
1 tablespoon lemon juice
1 level teaspoon salt
1 cucumber
8 tomatoes
1 onion
4 tablespoons water
a pinch of cayenne pepper
1 tablespoon capers
1 level teaspoon flour
1 tablespoon single cream

Preparation time: 15 minutes.
Cooking time: 20 minutes.

Rinse and dry the fish. Cut it into even-sized cubes, sprinkle with the lemon juice and salt, cover and leave for 10 minutes. Peel and halve the cucumber lengthwise, scraping the pips out with a teaspoon, then cut the cucumber halves into pieces. Wash the tomatoes and cut them into eight wedges. Peel and chop the onion. Put fish, with the lemon juice, cucumber pieces, tomato wedges, onion and water, into a saucepan, cover and cook over low heat for 20 minutes. 5 minutes before the end of the cooking time,

mix in the cayenne pepper and capers and cook for five minutes over low heat. Knead together butter and flour and whisk this mixture into the ragoût, letting it boil up once. Finally mix in the single cream.

Goes well with: plain boiled rice or plain boiled potatoes.

Steamed Halibut
△ ○

Approx. 200 calories per person

4 halibut fillets of 150g
    (5½oz) each
1 tablespoon lemon juice
1 level teaspoon salt
½ cup hot water

Preparation time: 25 minutes.
Cooking time: 20 minutes.

Wash and dry the fish fillets. Sprinkle them with the lemon juice and salt. Let marinate for about 10 minutes. Now put fish fillets with the lemon juice and the hot water into a shallow pan, cover and cook over low heat for 20 minutes.

49

Fish and Shellfish

Goes well with: potatoes in their jackets and 1 tablespoon butter per person (= 114 calories per person).

Peel and chop the onions finely, then mix with the peeled tomatoes, bay leaf, salt, pepper and oregano and spread evenly over the fish. Cook the fish in the oven for 40 minutes.

Goes well with: plain boiled rice or mashed potatoes.

Fish Fillets — Creole Fashion
△ ○ ○ *

Approx. 225 calories per person

1 tablespoon butter
800g (28oz) cod fillet
1 level tablespoon flour
1 small onion
500g (18oz) canned peeled tomatoes
1 bay leaf
1 level teaspoon salt
a pinch of pepper
¼ teaspoon dried oregano

Preparation time: 10 minutes.
Cooking time: 40 minutes.

Preheat oven to 177°C (350°F; gas mark 4). Grease a fireproof dish with the butter. Cut the fish into even-sized cubes and place them into the dish. Sprinkle the flour over the cubes.

Veal, Beef, Pork, Lamb

Calf's Liver – Berlin Fashion
△ △ ○ ○

Approx. 290 calories per person

4 slices calf's liver, each weighing 150g (5½oz)
2 apples
2 onions
2 tablespoons oil
½ teaspoon salt

Preparation time: 25 minutes.

Remove skin and gristle from the liver slices, rinse and dry them. Peel and core the apples and cut them into thick slices. Peel the onions and cut them into rings. Heat the oil in a pan and fry the liver slices in it for three minutes on each side, over fierce heat. Salt them after frying and place on a preheated dish to keep warm. Fry the apples and onion rings in the remaining fat. Finally, place the apples and onions on top of the liver.

Goes well with: mashed potatoes.

Veal Cutlet 'Broadway'
△ ○ ○

Approx. 225 calories per person

4 veal cutlets of 150g (5½oz) each
4 tomatoes
1 onion
1 tablespoon oil
½ teaspoon salt
a pinch each of pepper and dried oregano
1 tablespoon finely chopped parsley

Preparation time: 10 minutes.
Cooking time: 15 minutes.

Rinse and dry the veal cutlets, slightly cutting the edges at 3 cm (1″) intervals. Wash the tomatoes and cut them into eight wedges. Cut the peeled onion into rings. Heat the oil in a large frying-pan and fry the onion rings for about two minutes on either side, remove and dry them on kitchen paper. Fry the veal cutlets in the remaining oil over fierce heat for two minutes on each side. Place the onion rings on top of the cutlets and cover these with the tomatoes. Sprinkle the salt, pepper and oregano over the tomatoes. Cover the pan and cook over very low heat for 15 minutes. Finally, garnish with the parsley.

Goes well with: Potato Salad (recipe on page 93) or French bread.

Fricassée of Veal 'Prior'
△ ○ ○

Approx. 240 calories per person

500g (18oz) shoulder of veal
1 onion
1 tablespoon oil
¼ cup hot water
1 bay leaf
½ teaspoon salt
¼ teaspoon white pepper
3/8 litre (¾ pt) water
300g (11oz) deep-frozen peas
150g (5½oz) canned mushrooms
1 level tablespoon flour
4 tablespoons single cream
1 level teaspoon curry powder

Preparation time: 40 minutes.

Rinse the meat under cold water and cut into small even-sized cubes. Chop the peeled onion finely. Heat the oil in a saucepan, lightly brown the onion before adding the meat cubes and frying them on all sides.

51

Veal, Beef, Pork, Lamb

Now add ¼ cup of hot water, the bay leaf, salt and pepper, cover and stew over medium heat for 20 minutes. In the meantime heat the ³/₈ litre (¾ pt) water and add this after 20 minutes to the meat, together with the frozen peas and mushrooms and cook over medium heat for another ten minutes. Mix the flour with the cream and curry powder, add this mixture to the fricassée and stir until it comes once more to the boil.

Goes well with: white bread or plain boiled rice.

A hint: The fricassée can be further enriched by the addition of a small can of asparagus tips, making another 15 calories per person.

Calf's Tongue in Caper Sauce
△ ○ ○ *

Approx. 285 calories per person

½ litre (1 pt) water
500g (18oz) calf's tongue
1 small onion
3 cloves
½ bay leaf
½ teaspoon salt
¼ teaspoon pepper
1 level tablespoon flour
4 tablespoons single cream
1 egg yolk
some small capers
1 tablespoon butter
a pinch of sugar
a few drops lemon juice

Preparation time: 20 minutes.
Cooking time: 60 minutes.

Bring the water to the boil. Rinse the tongue under cold water and dry it. Cut the peeled onion into 8 wedges and put into the water together with the cloves, bay leaf, salt and pepper. Add the tongue to the boiling water, reduce the heat and simmer for 60 minutes. After that time, remove the tongue and strain the liquor. Skin the tongue, cutting off all sinews and gristle. Cut the tongue into even slices and keep warm. Now whisk the flour together with the

cream and egg yolk, adding a little of the hot liquor; stir this mixture into the rest of the liquor and let it come to the boil just once. The tongue and the capers are now put into the sauce and the butter added as well as the sugar and lemon juice to taste. Finally, reheat but don't let come to the boil again before serving.

Goes well with: toasted white bread and Melon Salad (recipe on page 94).

Escalopes of Veal with Peaches
△ △ ○ ○

Approx. 325 calories per person

4 veal escalopes of 160g (6oz) each
½ teaspoon celery salt
¼ teaspoon white pepper
1 level tablespoon flour
2 level teaspoons paprika
2 tablespoons oil
4 canned peach halves
4 tablespoons bitter orange liqueur
2 tablespoons brandy

Preparation time: 20 minutes.

Calf's Liver – Berlin Fashion, recipe on page 51 ▷

Veal, Beef, Pork, Lamb

Remove the sinews and skin from the escalopes and flatten them a little with the blade of a knife. Wash them quickly and dry them well. Mix together the celery salt, pepper, flour and paprika and pass the escalopes through this mixture. Heat the oil in a frying-pan and fry the escalopes in it for six minutes, turning them several times; keep them warm on a preheated dish. Cut the peach halves into slices of approximately 1 cm (³⁄₈″) and heat them in the left-over fat. Mix the liqueur

with the brandy, pour over the peaches, set carefully alight and let it burn out. Place the peaches at once on top of the escalopes.

Illustration below

Goes well with: mashed potatoes or French bread and peas.

Veal Scallops in Cream Sauce △ ○ ○ ○

Approx. 300 calories per person

600g (22oz) veal (for
*   escalopes)*
1 level tablespoon flour
1 onion
1 tablespoon oil
1 cup hot water
½ teaspoon salt
¼ cup of white wine
a pinch of sugar
a pinch of pepper
1 egg yolk
5 tablespoons cream

Escalopes of Veal with Peaches, recipe on page 52

Veal, Beef, Pork, Lamb

Preparation time: 30 minutes.

Remove all fat and gristle from the veal, cut into thin slices and pass it through the flour. Chop the peeled onion. Heat the oil in a stew-pan and fry the onions in it. Add the veal slices and fry them quickly for about 4 minutes, stirring all the time. Pour the hot water with the salt over the meat, cover and cook over low heat for 10 minutes. Add the white wine, let boil once, then reduce the heat. Whisk together the pepper, sugar, egg yolk and cream and stir this into the escalopes.

Goes well with: mashed potatoes and Brussels Sprouts Salad (recipe on page 90).

Calf's Sweetbread in Cream Sauce
△ ○ ○ ○

Approx. 215 calories per person

600g (22oz) calf's sweet-
    bread
³/8 litre (¾ pt) instant stock
a pinch each of salt and
    pepper
2 egg yolks

5 tablespoons single cream
1–2 tablespoons finely
    chopped parsley

Soaking time: 4 hours.
Preparation time: 25 minutes.

Soak the sweetbread for 4 hours in cold water. Then rinse it under cold water and put it in cold water, cover and let cook for four minutes over low heat. Take it out and rinse it with cold water; remove all skin and gristle and cut it into slices of about 2 cm (¾″) thickness. Put the sweetbread, the instant stock, salt and pepper into a saucepan, cover and cook over low heat for 15 minutes. Whisk the egg yolks and cream together, adding a little of the hot cooking liquor. Remove the sweetbread from the heat before stirring in the egg-cream mixture. Garnish with the chopped parsley.

Goes well with: plain boiled rice or mashed potatoes and Bean and Carrot Salad (recipe on page 94).

Calf's Kidney in Onion Sauce
△ ○ ○ *

Approx. 230 calories per person

500g (18oz) calf's kidneys
1 tablespoon oil
½ teaspoon salt
a pinch of pepper
1 onion
1/8 litre (¼ pt) instant stock
1 level tablespoon flour
¼ cup milk
2 tablespoons single cream
1 tablespoon chopped pars-
    ley

Preparation time: 35 minutes.
Cooking time: 20 minutes.

Halve the kidneys lengthwise, remove all sinews, tubes and fat, rinse them under cold water and soak them in cold milk or water for 30 minutes. Then rinse them again, dry and slice them. Heat the oil in a pan and fry the kidneys for 6–8 minutes, turning them constantly. Remove the kidneys, season them with salt and pepper and keep them warm. Peel, chop and lightly fry the onion in the remaining fat. Add the instant stock, stir and let boil once. Stir the cold milk into the flour, add this mixture to the sauce and stir until

Veal, Beef, Pork, Lamb

it comes once more to the boil. The cream and parsley are now stirred into the sauce before the kidney slices are returned to it to heat through over very gentle heat.

Goes well with: mashed potatoes and carrot salad bought in a jar.

Boiled Beef
△ ○ ○ * *

Approx. 320 calories per person

500g (18oz) beef (fore rib, brisket or topside)
a bunch of soup vegetables
1 onion
1 clove garlic
1½ litres (3 pt) water
1 level teaspoon salt

Preparation time: 15 minutes.
Cooking time: 2 hours.

Briefly rinse meat. Clean and wash the soup vegetables. Cut the peeled onion into 8 wedges. Peel the garlic. Bring the water with the salt, garlic, onion and soup vegetables to the boil; add the meat, cover and cook for two hours over low

heat. Remove the meat from the liquor and cut into slices. Arrange them and the vegetables on a serving dish.

Illustration on facing page

Goes well with: Potato Salad (recipe on page 93).

A recommendation: Season the meat broth to taste and keep for another meal when, after adding some garnish, you can serve it as a soup. Alternatively, you can freeze the stock, but in this case postpone the seasoning until reheating.

Beef Slices in Vegetable Sauce
△ ○ ○

Approx. 305 calories per person

2 onions
300g (11oz) tomatoes
1 tablespoon oil
4 slices of beef of 100g (3½oz) each (cut from the topside)
1 cup hot instant stock
1 pkt frozen soup vegetables
a pinch each of salt and pepper
a little horseradish to taste

Preparation time: 10 minutes.
Cooking time: 40 minutes.

Peel and dice the onions. Make slight incisions at the bottom-end of the tomatoes before pouring boiling water over them. Leave them in the water for a few minutes, then peel and cut them into small pieces. Heat the oil in a shallow pan and fry the meat slices quickly over strong heat. Pour the hot instant stock over them, add the tomatoes, onions and frozen soup vegetables and cook it all over very low heat for 35 minutes. Finally season the vegetable sauce with the salt, pepper and horseradish to taste.

Goes well with: wholemeal bread or plain boiled potatoes.

56

Boiled Beef, recipe on this page ▷

Veal, Beef, Pork, Lamb

Princely Tatar
△ ○ ○

Approx. 200 calories per person

500g (18oz) minced beef-steak (tatar)
2 egg yolks
2 onions
1 pickled cucumber
1 jar German caviar
salt
pepper
celery salt
paprika
tabasco sauce
brandy

Preparation time: 10 minutes.

Dress the minced steak on a dish, taking care that the texture remains undisturbed (see illustration below). Make 2 hollows into the meat with an egg, into which you put the egg yolks. Peel and chop the onion. Dice the pickled cucumber. Put the onions, cucumber, caviar and spices in separate small heaps around the meat. Serve the tabasco sauce and the brandy separately. Each

diner helps himself to some tatar and seasons his portion with whatever condiments on the platter he finds to his taste.

Illustration below

Goes well with: wholemeal bread or toast.

A possible alternative: You can mix the tatar with the condiments and spread it on thin slices of white bread, which you then serve as canapés, decorated with caviar substitute.

Princely Tatar, recipe above

Veal, Beef, Pork, Lamb

Garnished Steak
△ ○ ○

Approx. 275 calories per person

*4 rump steaks of 180g
  (6½oz) each
1 can asparagus tips 280g
  (10oz)
1 teaspoon butter
½ teaspoon salt
2 tomatoes
1 level teaspoon pepper
1 tablespoon oil*

Preparation time: 20 minutes.

Rinse and dry the steaks; lightly cut into the narrow fat edge at intervals of 2 cm (¾"). Drain the asparagus and heat it with the butter and the salt in a covered pan over low heat. Wash and slice tomatoes. Rub the steaks with the pepper. Heat the oil in a frying-pan and fry the steaks over medium heat for four minutes on each side. Add the tomatoes to the pan and heat through.

Place the steaks with the frying liquor on a dish with the tomato slices and asparagus tips as garnish.

Illustration below

Goes well with: French bread or parsley, or potatoes and green salad.

Garnished Steak, recipe above

Veal, Beef, Pork, Lamb

Roast Beéf 'à la Jardiniere'

△△○○○ * * *

Approx. 390 calories per person

1 carrot
½ leek
500g (18oz) beef (topside or sirloin)
½ teaspoon salt
½ teaspoon white pepper
6–7 tablespoons hot water
2 tablespoons butter
4 tomatoes
½ teaspoon onion salt

1 tablespoon finely chopped chives
a small bunch of parsley
some paprika

Preparation time: 35 minutes.

Preheat the oven to 250°C (500°F; gas mark 9). Scrape and wash the carrot and cut it into thin strips. Halve the leek lengthwise, wash it thoroughly and cut it into thin slices. Briefly rinse the meat, dry and rub it with the salt and pepper. Place it, fat side down, into a roasting pan. Pour 3 tablespoons hot water round the meat; surround it with the carrots and leek. Heat the butter and pour over the meat. Place the meat into the preheated oven (second shelf from the bottom) and roast for 16–20 minutes (after 16 minutes the meat will still be red inside, after 20 minutes it will have become pink). Wash and slice the tomatoes, and add them after 12 minutes cooking time to the meat to let them cook with it. Baste the meat once or twice. When it is

Roast Beef 'à la Jardinière', recipe above

Veal, Beef, Pork, Lamb

done, turn off the oven but leave the roasting pan in to rest the meat for another ten minutes. Then place the meat on a preheated dish and cut it across the fibres, into slices. Put the tomatoes on and around the meat and season with the onion salt and chives. Garnish with the parsley. De-glaze the pan, that is: dilute the concentrated juices in the pan with 3–4 tablespoons of water, add a little salt, pepper and paprika to taste and pour with the vegetables over the meat.

Illustration on facing page

Goes well with: French bread and any salad.

A piece of advice: A more economical and better roast can be obtained by roasting 1kg (2¼lb) meat at one go instead of only 500g (18oz), which is the quantity needed for four persons. In order not to exceed the calories stated at the top of this recipe, you serve only half the meat. The other half is left to be eaten cold in sandwiches or with a curd-cheese remoulade sauce, or to be deep-frozen for another occasion.

Tatar Steak in a Piquant Sauce
△ ○ ○ *

Approx. 155 calories per person

450g (16oz) tatar (best minced beefsteak)
1 level teaspoon salt
¼ teaspoon pepper
1 tablespoon oil
½ cup canned tomato juice
dietetic sweetener (equivalent to ½ teaspoon sugar)
1 teaspoon lemon juice
½ teaspoon mustard
1 teaspoon barbecue sauce (ready-bought product)

Preparation time: 25 minutes.

Season the minced beefsteak with the salt and pepper, shaping from it 4 or 8 small flat cakes. Heat the oil in a frying-pan and lightly brown the meat cakes on both sides. Stir together the tomato juice, the sweetener, lemon juice, mustard and barbecue sauce, add this mixture to the rissoles and continue the cooking process for a few more minutes over low heat. To serve, carefully remove the meat rissoles from the pan, place them on a dish and surround with the sauce.

Goes well with: mashed potatoes and green salad.

Shepherd's Roast
△ △ ○ ○ ○

Approx. 250 calories per person

1 bread roll
1 cup water
1 onion
15 stuffed olives
1 egg
2 level tablespoons white breadcrumbs
1 teaspoon capers
1 teaspoon mustard
½ teaspoon black pepper
a pinch of ground ginger
a pinch of ground nutmeg
½ teaspoon salt
2 tablespoons finely chopped parsley
400g (14oz) minced beefsteak (tatar)
1 tablespoon oil

Preparation time: 25 minutes.
Cooking time: 35 minutes.

Slice the bread roll and soak in the water. Peel and finely dice onion. Dice olives as well. Squeeze out the roll

61

Veal, Beef, Pork, Lamb

and mix with the egg, bread-crumbs, onions, capers, mustard, pepper, ginger, nutmeg, salt, parsley and the minced beefsteak. Preheat the oven to 220°C (425°F; gas mark 7). Shape the meat mixture into a high, oblong loaf. Brush a baking sheet lightly with oil, put the loaf on it and sprinkle the rest of the oil over the loaf. Bake for 35 minutes on the middle shelf of the oven. If, after 20 minutes, the top is too brown cover with foil for the rest of the cooking time.

Illustration below

Goes well with: chicory salad with tomatoes and rye-bread.

Piquant Ox Liver
△ ○ ○

Approx. 280 calories per person

600g (22oz) ox liver
1 onion
1 tablespoon oil
1 level tablespoon flour
¼ litre (½ pt) water
½ teaspoon salt
¼ teaspoon pepper
a pinch of dried marjoram
1/16 litre (1/8 pt 2½oz)
*   soured cream*

Preparation time: 1½ hours.

Shepherd's Roast, recipe above
Colourful Pork Skewers, recipe on page 64 ▷

Veal, Beef, Pork, Lamb

Remove sinews and skin from the liver, cut into small even slices and put it in salted water to soak for an hour. Peel, chop and lightly fry the onion in the heated oil; add the liver and fry quickly for 4–5 minutes, turning the slices continuously. Dust over the flour and let quickly brown. Add the water and season with the salt and pepper; cover and cook for about 8 minutes over a low heat. Mix the marjoram and soured cream into the sauce.

Goes well with: parsley potatoes and carrot salad.

Beef Stroganoff
△○○○ * *

Approx. 280 calories per person

1 onion
2 tablespoons butter
1 level tablespoon flour
1 cup instant stock
½ teaspoon mustard
½ teaspoon salt
¼ teaspoon pepper
600g (22oz) fillet of beef
3 tablespoons sour cream

Preparation time: 30 minutes.

Peel and chop the onion. Melt half the butter in a pan, add the flour, stir until light brown and then work in the stock. Dissolve the mustard in it and stir until a smooth sauce is obtained. Season with the salt and pepper. Cut the fillet into small even-sized pieces. Heat the rest of the butter in a frying-pan and fry the onions, add the meat and fry quickly on all sides. Put the meat, together with onions, into the sauce, cover and cook slowly for 15 minutes. Just before serving, add the sour cream to the sauce.

Goes well with: French bread or plain boiled potatoes and Green Salad (recipe on page 93).

Colourful Pork Skewers
△ △ ○

Approx. 370 calories per person

600g (22oz) fillet of pork
1 level teaspoon salt
½ teaspoon pepper
a pinch of ground cloves
4 tomatoes
2 apples
1 teaspoon mustard
1 level teaspoon paprika
1 level teaspoon sugar
1 tablespoon wine vinegar
2 tablespoons oil (olive oil for preference)
10 stoned green olives
½ onion

Preparation time: 40 minutes.

Rinse and dry the meat and cut it into even-sized cubes. Preheat the oven to 175°C (350°F; gas mark 4). Mix together half the salt and pepper as well as the ground cloves. Wash and slice tomatoes. Wash, core and slice the apples. Take 4 skewers and spike on each of them in turn: a meat cube, a tomato and an apple slice, and so on till the spikes are full; sprinkle the mixed condiments over them and put on an oiled baking sheet to cook in the oven for 30 minutes, turning them repeatedly. Mix together the

Veal, Beef, Pork, Lamb

mustard, paprika, sugar, the remaining salt and pepper, the vinegar and oil. Finely chop the olives and onion, add them to the sauce and heat through stirring all the time. Serve the sauce separately.

Illustration on page 63

Goes well with: mashed potatoes.

Pork Fillet 'en croûte'
△ △ ○ ○

Approx. 375 calories per person

*1 packet of frozen puff
  pastry (300g = 11oz)
400g (14oz) fillet of pork
  in a piece
¼ teaspoon salt
¼ teaspoon paprika*

Defrosting time: 4 hours.
Cooking time: 45 minutes.

Defrost the puff pastry at room temperature (approximately 4 hours) then roll it out to a thickness of about ½ cm (³⁄₁₆"). Preheat the oven to 180°C (350°F; gas mark 4). Rinse the pork and dry it well. Rub the fillet with the salt and paprika and let it rest for ten minutes. Wrap the meat in the rolled-out pastry, damping the pastry edges with water to seal. Prick the top of the pastry several

Pork Fillet 'en croûte', recipe above

Veal, Beef, Pork, Lamb

times. Rinse a baking sheet under cold water, put the pork in its puff-pastry envelope on it and bake on the middle shelf of the preheated oven for 30 minutes.

Illustration on page 65

Goes well with: canned beetroot and white bread.

Fillet of Lamb with Girolles
△ ○ ○ ○

Approx. 400 calories per person

4 slices of fillet of lamb, weighing 100g (3½oz) each

1 tablespoon oil
½ teaspoon salt
½ teaspoon black pepper
2 slices toasting bread
1 tablespoon butter
50g (2oz) of canned girolles
½ cup instant gravy
½ cup Madeira wine
65g (2½oz) canned liver pâté

Preparation time: 30 minutes.

Briefly rinse and dry the lamb fillets; heat the oil in a frying-pan and fry them for 4 minutes on each side. Season with salt and pepper and keep warm on a preheated dish. Cut the bread slices diagonally and fry

them in the oil until crispy brown on both sides. Keep them warm as well. Add the butter to the oil to heat the girolles over moderate heat. Prepare the gravy according to the instructions on the packet. Mix ½ cup of this sauce with the Madeira. Pour this mixture over the girolles and heat through. Cut the liver pâté into 4 slices.

To serve, place each fillet on a piece of bread, garnish with a slice of liver pâté and pour the girolles with their sauce around it.

Illustration below

Goes well with: tomato — or green — salad.

Fillet of Lamb with Girolles, recipe above

Veal, Beef, Pork, Lamb

Pork and Vegetable Ragoût
△ ○ ○

Approx. 300 calories per person

500g (18oz) pork fillet
½ teaspoon salt
¼ teaspoon pepper
a pinch of cayenne
1 red pepper
4 tomatoes
300g (11oz) frozen beans
1 level tablespoon flour
1 tablespoon butter or margarine

Preparation time: 30 minutes.
Cooking time: 60 minutes.

Rinse and quickly dry the meat and cut it into 2 cm (¾") cubes. Put the meat, with the salt, pepper and cayenne into a pan, adding sufficient water to cover it and cook for 60 minutes over low heat with the lid on. Halve the pepper, removing pips and ribs, wash and cut it into strips. Make a crosswise incision at the bottom-end of the tomatoes, pour boiling water over them, leave a few minutes, then peel and cut them into eight wedges. When the meat has cooked for 30 minutes, add the pepper strips to it. After a further 20 minutes, add the tomatoes and frozen beans. When the meat is done, blend the flour with cold water, stir into the meat broth and bring to the boil just once. Season the dish to taste with a little vinegar, salt and cayenne pepper and finally add the butter.

Goes well with: plain boiled potatoes.

Leg of Mutton
△ ○ ○

Approx. 380 calories per person

400g (14oz) leg of mutton
1 level teaspoon salt
a good pinch of pepper
a sprig of chervil
8 small potatoes
500g (18oz) frozen beans
a pinch of powdered garlic
¼ cup instant stock
1 tablespoon butter, flaked

Preparation time: 25 minutes.
Cooking time: 50 minutes.

Put an unglazed fireproof dish into cold water for ten minutes. Rinse and quickly dry the meat. Mix half the salt with the pepper. Wash and drain the chervil. Peel and wash the potatoes. Drain the dish. Rub the meat with the seasoning, put it into the dish and place the chervil on top. Surround the meat with the beans and potatoes and sprinkle with the rest of the salt and the garlic powder. Pour the instant stock over the vegetables and top the whole with the butter flakes. Cover the dish and put on the lowest shelf of the oven. Cook the leg for 50 minutes at 250°C (500°F, gas mark 9) and serve in the cooking dish.

Goes well with: Coffee Mousse (recipe on page 110).

Game and Poultry

Haunch of Venison
△△○○○ * *

Approx. 320 calories per person

800g (28oz) haunch of venison
1 onion
100g (3½oz) fat bacon thinly sliced
½ teaspoon salt
a pinch each of pepper and ground coriander
200g (7oz) canned girolles (wild mushrooms)

Preparation time: 20 minutes.
Cooking time: 140 minutes.

This dish requires an unglazed earthenware pot, called 'Roman Pot', which enables you to cook food in its own juice without adding any liquid. The Roman Pot is left lying in cold water for ten minutes, during which time you rub the haunch of venison with a cloth which you've soaked in vinegar. Remove all sinews and skins. Peel the onion and cut into eighths.

The Roman Pot is now drained and lined with half the bacon slices. Rub the salt, pepper and coriander into the meat before placing on the bacon slices. The girolles are placed around the meat. The remaining bacon slices are put on top of the meat; the lid is put on the pot and it's then placed on the lowest shelf of the oven. The oven is now heated to a temperature of 245°C (500°F; gas mark 9) — food to be cooked in a Roman Pot should never be placed in a preheated oven.

Haunch of Venison, recipe above

After 2 hours take off the lid, remove the bacon on top and allow the roast to brown in the switched-off oven. Now take the roast out of the Roman Pot and onto a flat dish, and slice and sprinkle the girolles over the slices (the bacon should not be eaten).

Illustration on facing page

Goes well with: grilled tomatoes and boiled potatoes.

Rabbit Ragoût Bordeaux Fashion
△ ○ ○

Approx. 280 calories per person

600g (21oz) rabbit pieces
1 onion
1 tablespoon oil
1 cup hot water
1 bay leaf
2 peppercorns
½ teaspoon salt
a pinch of pepper
1 level tablespoon flour
½ cup red wine
2 tablespoons canned milk

Preparation time: 40 minutes.

Rub thoroughly the rabbit pieces with a cloth soaked in vinegar, removing sinews and skins, and cut into cubes of even size. Peel and dice onion. Heat oil in a stewing pan and in it fry lightly the diced onion and the rabbit pieces, turning them constantly. The hot water is poured over the meat and the bay leaf, peppercorns, salt and pepper are added. Cover the pan and let the meat cook over low heat for 20 to 25 minutes. Stir the flour in a little cold water, add to the ragoût and let it come to the boil once while stirring it all the while. Now remove the ragoût from the fire, stir the red wine and milk into it and heat up once more but don't let it come to the boil.

Goes well with: potato purée and beetroots from a jar.

Leg of Hare
△ ○ ○

Approx. 240 calories per person

1 leg of hare (600g/21oz)
1 level teaspoon salt
½ teaspoon pepper
½ litre (1 pt) buttermilk
1 tablespoon oil

⅛ litre (¼ pt) instant meat stock
¼ bay leaf
2 juniper berries
1 glass brandy

Marinating time: 2 hours.
Cooking time: 40 minutes.
Preparation time: 5 minutes.

Rub the leg of hare with a cloth soaked in vinegar, then rub in the salt and pepper. Pour the buttermilk over it, cover and let marinate for 4 hours. Heat the oil in a stewing pan. Take the leg of hare out of the marinade, dab dry and fry briskly in the oil. Fill up with the instant meat stock, bay leaf and juniper berries, cover and let the meat stew over low heat for 40 minutes. Measure off ¼ litre (½pt) buttermilk and stir into the sauce together with the brandy just before serving.

Goes well with: mashed potatoes and red cabbage.

Escalope of Venison in Tomato Sauce
△ ○ ○ ○

Approx. 230 calories per person

4 escalopes of venison of 150g (5½oz) each

Game and Poultry

½ teaspoon salt
½ teaspoon pepper
1 level tablespoon flour
1 tablespoon oil
3 tablespoons tomato purée
1 level tablespoon paprika
³/8 litre (¾ pt) water
¹/16 litre (¹/8 pt) soured
    cream

Preparation time: 30 minutes.

Rub the escalopes with a cloth soaked in vinegar and thereafter with the salt. Mix the pepper with the flour and turn the escalopes in it. Heat the oil in a frying-pan and fry the meat on both sides for 8 minutes over medium heat. Place the escalopes on a preheated serving dish and keep warm. Whisk together the tomato purée with the remaining flour, the paprika and water, pour this mixture into the frying-pan, stir to loosen the juice from the frying process and bring to boil once more. Stir the soured cream into the sauce and pour over the escalopes.

Goes well with: mashed potatoes and peas.

Braised Haunch of Venison
△ ○ ○ ○

Approx. 280 calories per person

600g (21oz) haunch of
    venison, boned
1 onion
½ carrot
¼ celeriac
¹/8 litre (¼ pt) red wine
¹/8 litre (¼ pt) water
½ bay leaf
2 juniper berries
1 clove
1 or 2 drops of a dietary
    sweetener (equivalent
    to 1 teaspoon sugar)
1 tablespoon oil
150g (5½oz) fresh mush-
    rooms
½ cup shredded pineapple
¹/16 litre (¹/8 pt) soured
    cream
½ teaspoon salt
¼ teaspoon pepper

Preparation time: 10 minutes.
Marinating time: 3 hours.
Cooking time: 40 minutes.

Remove all skins and sinews from the venison before rubbing it thoroughly on all sides with a cloth soaked in vinegar. Peel and dice onion. Scrape and wash the carrot and cut into batons. Peel celeriac thickly and cut into pieces. Let the red wine, water, bay leaf, juniper berries, clove and sweetener cook for 5 minutes with the vegetables and then pour the lot over the venison. The meat is now covered and allowed to marinate for three hours. Take the venison out of the marinade and dab dry. Pass the marinade through a sieve, keeping ³/16 litre (³/8 pt) for later use. Heat oil thoroughly in a stewing pan and fry the venison briskly on all sides. Pour the marinade over the meat, cover and let cook for 30 minutes over low heat. Clean mushrooms, wash and cut them into slices. Ten minutes before the meat is done, add the mushrooms and the shredded pineapple to the liquor. Place the venison on a preheated flat dish and slice the meat. The soured cream together with the salt and pepper is stirred into the gravy, which is served separately.

Goes well with: mashed potatoes and preserved beetroot.

Chicken Roasted in a 'Roman Pot', recipe on page 72 ▷

Game and Poultry

Chicken Roasted in a 'Roman Pot'
△ △ ○

Approx. 505 calories per person

1 chicken of about 1kg (2¼lb), oven-ready (may be deep-frozen)
½ teaspoon salt
½ teaspoon paprika
1 green pepper
100 g (3½oz) celery
1 leek
2 carrots
1 onion
100g (3½oz) rice
½ teaspoon pepper

Preparation time: 20 minutes (deep-frozen chicken must be allowed to thaw before).
Cooking time: 1½ hours.

The pot required for this dish is an unglazed earthenware ovenproof container called a 'Roman Pot'. You place the pot 10 minutes in cold water (the undoubted advantage of the Roman Pot is that what you cook in it doesn't require the addition of any liquid, thus allowing the food to cook in its own juices). Wash chicken inside and out under running cold water, dab dry and rub the inside with salt and paprika. Clean and wash vegetables, cutting pepper into strips, the celery into dice and the leek, carrots and onions into slices. Wash rice in a sieve and drain. Place the chicken with the rice and vegetables into the Roman Pot, cover and place on the lowest shelf of a cold oven, set oven temperature to 250°C (475°F; gas mark 9) and let the chicken cook for 1½ hours. Carve chicken, place rice and vegetables on a dish and arrange the chicken pieces on top.

Illustration of chicken still in the Roman Pot on page 71

Chicken Breasts Royal
△ ○ ○ ○

Approx. 260 calories per person

250g (9oz) fresh mushrooms
1 green pepper
1 red pepper
1 cup instant chicken stock
600g (22oz) deep-frozen chicken breasts
1 egg yolk
4 tablespoons single cream
a pinch each of salt and pepper
a liqueur glass of sherry
125g (4½oz) canned truffles

Preparation time: 15 minutes.
Cooking time: 30 minutes.

The mushrooms are cleaned, washed thoroughly and finely sliced. The peppers are quartered and the pips removed before being washed and cut into strips. Bring the instant chicken stock to the boil. Place the deep-frozen chicken breasts into the stock, cover them with the sliced mushrooms and the pepper strips, cover and braise them over low heat for 25 minutes. Whisk together the egg yolk, single cream, salt and pepper, add a little of the liquor to this mixture and stir it all into the braised chicken. Remove saucepan from the heat and add the sherry to the sauce to taste. If necessary cut the truffles into smaller pieces, distribute them over the chicken breasts and serve.

Goes well with: toast or boiled rice.

Game and Poultry

Chicken Liver on Toast
△ ○

Approx. 300 calories per person

500g (18oz) chicken liver
1 tablespoon oil
a pinch each of salt and pepper
1 onion
½ cup instant gravy
4 tablespoons very finely sliced mushrooms
2 tablespoons single cream
1 teaspoon butter
4 slices starch-reduced toast
1 tablespoon chopped parsley

Preparation time: 20 minutes.

Remove any sinews or odd bits of fat from the chicken liver. Heat oil and fry the chicken liver in it for 8 minutes, turning it all the while. Remove liver from frying-pan, salt and pepper it and keep it warm. Peel, dice and lightly fry the onion in the remaining oil, stirring constantly. Pour the gravy over the onions and warm up over slow heat. Add the mushrooms and the single cream to the sauce, stirring it and warm up, but without letting it boil. Melt the butter in the frying-pan and fry the slices of toast in it on one side only.

Put the slices of toast on four individual plates, spread the chicken liver over them, pour the gravy over the toast and sprinkle them with parsley.

Goes well with: sweet-sour cucumber salad or American Cucumber Salad (recipe on page 95).

Chicken with Curried Curd Cheese
△ △ ○ ○

Approx. 500 calories per person

1 young chicken, weighing about 1200g (approximately 2¾lb)
1 litre (almost 2 pt) water
¼ packet dried soup vegetables (or 1 onion, 1 carrot, a stick of celery, 1 leek)
1 level teaspoon salt
1 tablespoon oil
1 beaker yoghurt from skimmed milk
1 tablespoon butter
50g (2oz) curd cheese from skimmed milk
½ teaspoon curry powder

Preparation and cooking time: 70 minutes.

Wash the chicken thoroughly with cold water inside and out, then bring to the boil in the litre of water. Skim the impurities as soon as they appear, reduce the heat and repeat the skimming process several times. Add the soup vegetables and salt and continue cooking for another 40 minutes. Preheat the oven to a temperature of 200°C (400°F; gas mark 6). Lift the chicken out of the broth, cut it into 4 portions and rub these with oil. Brush a piece of aluminium foil with oil, place it on a baking sheet and put the chicken pieces in it. Push the baking tin onto the middle shelf of the oven and allow the chicken pieces to roast for 20 minutes, by which time they should be light brown. Stir the yoghurt together with the butter, curd cheese and curry powder and warm up over low heat, stirring constantly. Arrange the chicken portions on a serving dish and serve the curried curd cheese separately.

Illustration on page 74

Goes well with: boiled rice or sticks of French bread.

Game and Poultry

Fricassée of Chicken
△ ○ ○

Approx. 355 calories per person

1 roasting chicken, weighing about 800g (between 1¾ and 2lb)
1 carrot
1 onion
½ leek
¼ celeriac
½ litre (1 pt) water
1 level teaspoon salt
1 level tablespoon flour
2 tablespoons cold water
100g (3½oz) canned asparagus tips
100g (3½oz) deep-frozen peas
2 egg yolks
a pinch of grated nutmeg
2 tablespoons single cream

Cooking time: 70 minutes.
Preparation time: 25 minutes.

Briefly rinse roasting chicken inside and out under running cold water and cut it into 4 portions. Clean and scrape the carrot and cut into batons. Peel onion and cut it into eighths. Halve the leek lengthwise, wash it thoroughly and cut it into small pieces. Thoroughly brush the celeríac, then peel it thickly and wash and cut it into small pieces. Place the chicken portions with the water, salt, carrot pieces, onion eighths, leek and celery pieces into a saucepan, cover and cook over low heat for 45 minutes. The chicken done, put the entire contents of the saucepan through a sieve and let the broth get cold.

Chicken with Curried Curd Cheese, recipe on page 73

Bone the chicken pieces, removing any skin and cut them into small bite-size cubes. Skim the fat off the by now cold chicken broth, put it together with the chicken cubes into a saucepan and heat it up again. Stir the flour in the cold water before adding it to the chicken broth, which should be allowed to boil until the sauce begins to thicken. Next, the asparagus tips and the deep-frozen peas are added to the chicken fricassée which is then covered and heated through over low heat for 6 minutes. The egg yolks are stirred together with the grated nutmeg and the single cream, the fricassée removed from the fire and the egg yolk-cream mixture added to the dish which should be served at once.

Goes well with: toast and Savoury Chicory Salad (recipe on page 91).

Roast Pigeons with Mushroom Sauce
△ ○ ○ ○

Approx. 350 calories per person

4 young pigeons
1 level teaspoon salt
½ teaspoon white pepper
50g (2oz) thinly sliced
  bacon
1 cup hot instant meat
  stock
115g (4oz) canned mush-
  rooms
½ cup milk
1 level tablespoon flour
2 tablespoons soured cream

Preparation time: 10 minutes.
Cooking time: 55 minutes.

Preheat the oven to 225°C (425°F; gas mark 7). Rinse the inside and outside of the pigeons thoroughly in cold water, dab dry and rub the salt and pepper into them. Place them in an oven-proof dish or in a frying-pan, cover with the bacon slices and pour the hot instant meat stock over them. Put the container on the middle shelf of the oven and let them roast for 45 minutes, leaving them for another ten minutes in the switched-off oven. Pour the gravy into a pot, removing the bacon slices. Drain the

mushrooms in a sieve. The mushroom liquor is mixed with the milk and the flour whisked into it. This mixture is now stirred into the gravy and allowed to come to the boil once. Now add the mushrooms to the sauce to warm them up over low heat, but not to boil. Add the soured cream to the gravy. The pigeons are served on a platter with the sauce.

Goes well with: sticks of French bread and Braised Peppers (recipe on page 83).

Vegetables and Salads

Asparagus Bundles
△ △ ○ ○

Approx. 165 calories per person

2 kg (4½lb) asparagus
1 level teaspoon salt
1 lump sugar
4 eggs
1 green pepper

Preparation time: 45 minutes.

Peel the asparagus, cutting off the woody ends. In a rather large saucepan bring plenty of water to the boil, having added the salt and sugar; place the asparagus into it and cook over medium heat for 25 minutes. Boil the eggs for 10 minutes; cut the pepper into rings, removing pips, wash and drain it. Rinse the eggs under cold water, peel and slice them. Place on each of four individual serving dishes a white napkin on which to place the asparagus. Each portion of asparagus is now 'bundled' with the pepper rings. The egg slices are used to decorate the dish.

Illustration on facing page

Goes well with: melted butter (1 tablespoon per person = 114 calories),

chopped parsley, paprika and toast.

A tip: The asparagus liquor may be used together with the cut-off ends of the asparagus to make a soup.

Stuffed Peppers
△ ○ ○ * *

Approx. 235 calories per person

4 medium-sized red or
*   green peppers*
400g (14oz) minced steak
2 eggs
a pinch of garlic salt
½ teaspoon salt
¼ teaspoon paprika
2 tablespoons oil
¼ litre (½ pt) canned to-
*   mato juice*

Preparation time: 30 minutes.
Cooking time: 20 minutes.

Cut off the upper third of the peppers to use them as lids; remove the pips from the inside, wash thoroughly and put them on a grid to drain. Mix the minced beef with the eggs, garlic salt, salt, paprika and about 3 tablespoons of water until the mixture is smooth. Fill

it into the peppers, letting little heaps show above the rim. Put the lids on. Heat the oil in a shallow saucepan, place the peppers upright into it and lightly fry for about 5 minutes. Then pour the tomato juice around the peppers, cover and let cook over low heat for 20 minutes.

Illustration on page 79

Goes well with: boiled rice or wholemeal bread.

Brussels Sprouts with Onions
△ ○ * *

Approx. 115 calories per person

1 kilogram (2¼lb) Brussels
*   sprouts*
2 onions
½ teaspoon salt
½ cup hot water
1 tablespoon oil
1 tablespoon single cream
1 egg yolk
a generous pinch of grated
*   nutmeg*

Preparation time: 20 minutes.

76

Asparagus Bundles, recipe on this page ▷

Vegetables and Salads

Clean the Brussels sprouts, removing any imperfect and large leaves so that only small sprouts remain. Peel onions and cut into rings. The Brussels sprouts are now put into hot water together with the salt. The saucepan is covered and the sprouts are steamed for ten minutes over low heat. Heat the oil in another shallow saucepan and fry the onion rings in it until soft, stirring all the time. Add the sprouts with the liquid to the onion rings, mix well, cover and stew for a further 10 minutes over low heat. Whisk together the cream, egg yolk and grated nutmeg and stir the mixture into the vegetable before serving.

Goes well with: boiled beef and boiled potatoes.

A hint: The left-over sprouts could be used for the Brussels Sprouts Salad (recipe on page 90). If this dish is to be deep-frozen, don't add the cream-egg yolk mixture and the grated nutmeg until the dish is about to be served.

Leeks with a Cheese Sauce
△ ○ ○

Approx. 170 calories per person

6 leeks
½ cup hot water
½ teaspoon salt
⅛ litre (¼pt) instant meat stock
2 wedges processed cheese
1 level teaspoon cornflour
⅛ litre (¼pt) milk
a pinch each of pepper and grated nutmeg
1 tablespoon butter

Preparation time: 30 minutes.

Remove imperfect outer leaves from the leeks and cut off the root ends; cut the leeks into 5cm (2") long pieces. Wash them thoroughly under cold water and drain them. Put the leek pieces, together with the hot water and the salt into a saucepan, cover and steam them for about 15 minutes. Heat the instant meat stock, cut the processed cheese into small pieces and add them to the stock until the cheese is melted. Mix the cornflour with a little milk, add this mixture to the cheese sauce and slowly pour the cold milk into it. Bring the sauce to the boil several times, stirring all the while. Season it with the pepper and nutmeg to taste and finally melt the butter in it. Drain the leek pieces, put them into a dish and serve the cheese sauce separately.

Illustration on page 80

Cucumber Fricassée
△ ○ ○

Approx. 290 calories per person

1 large cucumber
50g (2oz) butter
2 tablespoons wine vinegar
¼ litre (½pt) instant meat stock
1 level tablespoon flour
1 level teaspoon salt
½ teaspoon white pepper
200g (7oz) very lean boiled ham
1 egg yolk
2 tablespoons chopped dill

Preparation time: 30 minutes.

Stuffed Peppers, recipe on page 76

Vegetables and Salads

Wash, peel and thinly slice cucumber. Melt the butter in a rather large saucepan and briefly fry the cucumber slices in it stirring all the time. Pour the vinegar and the instant meat stock over the cucumber slices, cover and bring to the boil. Sprinkle the flour over the cucumber, stir briefly, add the salt and pepper, cover and cook for a few minutes. Cut the ham into even-sized cubes, add them to the cucumber and heat them up over very low heat for about 10 minutes. Mix the egg yolk with a little of the cucumber liquor, remove the pot from the stove, gently stir the egg yolk mixture into the vegetable and finally sprinkle the dill over the fricassée.

Illustration below

Goes well with: boiled potatoes.

Fennel with Parmesan
△ ○ * *

Approx. 140 calories per person

4 rather small fennels
4 tablespoons water
½ teaspoon salt
½ beaker yoghurt from skimmed milk
a generous pinch of paprika
a pinch of white pepper
3 level tablespoons Parmesan cheese

Preparation time: 40 minutes.

Cucumber Fricassée, recipe above
◁ Leeks with a Cheese Sauce, recipe on page 78

Vegetables and Salads

Clean and wash the fennels and cut them into eighths; put them, together with the water and the salt, into a saucepan, cover and let steam for 30 minutes over low heat. Stir together the yoghurt, paprika and pepper and mix into the fennel. Sprinkle the Parmesan cheese over the vegetables.

Goes well with: escalope of veal nature and white bread.

A tip: If the dish is to be deep-frozen, add the Parmesan cheese only when defreezing and heating it.

Tender Carrots
△ ○ * * *

Approx. 135 calories per person

750g (27oz) young carrots
1 cup instant meat stock
2 tablespoons butter
4 tablespoons single cream
½ teaspoon sugar
4 tablespoons tomato juice

Preparation time: 55 minutes.

Brush the carrots under cold running water, cut them into batons, put them, together with the instant meat stock, in a saucepan, cover and steam over low heat for 30 minutes. The carrots done, add the butter. Mix together the single cream, sugar and tomato juice, stir into the carrots and bring once more to the boil.

Illustration below

82

Tender Carrots, recipe above

Vegetables and Salads

Curried Cucumber
△ ○

Approx. 80 calories per person

1½ cups water
a pinch of salt
1 large fresh cucumber
3 large onions
2 level tablespoons flour
¼ cup milk
½ – 1 teaspoon curry powder
1 tablespoon butter or margarine
a pinch of pepper

Preparation time: 20 minutes.

Bring the water with the salt to the boil. Peel the cucumber, halve it lengthways, removing the seeds with a teaspoon, and cut the cucumber halves into pieces of even size. Peel the onions and cut them into eighths. Put the cucumber pieces and the onion eighths into the boiling water, cover and cook over low heat for 5 to 8 minutes. Stir together the flour, milk and curry powder, add these to the vegetables and bring to the boil once or twice, stirring constantly, until the mixture begins to thicken. Now add the butter or margarine and the pepper; mix well and serve.

Goes well with: boiled beef or escalope of veal nature and boiled potatoes.

Braised Peppers
△ ○ * *

Approx. 110 calories per person

4 large peppers
1 cup boiling water
3 tablespoons butter
a generous pinch each of salt and pepper

Preparation time: 15 minutes.

Cut the peppers into eighths, removing the seeds; wash and put them into a saucepan, pour the boiling water over them, cover and cook them over low heat for 5 minutes. Drain the peppers in a sieve. Melt the butter in the saucepan and lightly fry the pepper pieces on all sides until light brown. Season with the salt and pepper.

Goes well with: Grilled Halibut (recipe on page 40) and mashed potatoes.

Stuffed Tomatoes
△ ○ ○ *

Approx. 175 calories per person

1 large onion
8 medium-sized tomatoes
400g (14oz) minced prime beef
1 egg
½ teaspoon salt
¼ teaspoon pepper
a pinch of dried oregano
1 tablespoon butter or margarine
½ cup water

Preparation time: 25 minutes.

Peel and dice the onion. Wash the tomatoes and cut off the tops for later use as lids. Hollow them out, keeping the flesh. Mix the minced beef with the diced onion, egg, salt, pepper and oregano; fill this mixture into the tomatoes and replace the lids. Melt the butter or margarine in a shallow saucepan, mix in the tomato flesh, add the water and heat. Place the tomatoes in the saucepan, cover and stew for 20 minutes over medium heat.

Goes well with: boiled rice or mashed potatoes.

Vegetables and Salads

Cabbage and Tomato Danburry
△ * *

Approx. 70 calories per person

4 tomatoes
½ small white cabbage
1 cup water
½ teaspoon salt
¼ teaspoon pepper
1½ teaspoons caraway seeds
1 tablespoon butter
*   or margarine*
1 level tablespoon flour

Preparation time: 30 minutes.

Make a few incisions at the bottom end of the tomatoes, pour some boiling water over them, let them lie for a few minutes in the hot water and then peel them. Remove any imperfect leaves from the cabbage, cut the hard stalk out and slice. Bring the water with the salt to the boil, put the sliced cabbage in as well as the tomatoes, cut in eighths, cover and cook for 10 minutes over low heat. The cabbage done, add the pepper and the caraway seeds. Knead the butter or margarine together with the flour and stir into the vegetable until dissolved. Bring to the boil once, then cover

and let stand for a few minutes.

Goes well with: boiled beef and boiled potatoes.

Asparagus in Cream Sauce
△ ○ ○ ○

Approx. 130 calories per person

500g (18oz) fresh asparagus
½ teaspoon salt
a pinch of sugar
¼ cup hot water
½ teaspoon lemon juice
⅛ litre (¼ pt) cream
a pinch of white pepper

Preparation time: 35 minutes.

The asparagus is peeled, the woody ends cut off, washed and cut into 4cm (1¾") pieces. The pieces are now put, together with the salt, sugar, and hot water, into a saucepan and steamed over low heat for 25 minutes. The cooked asparagus is drained in a sieve and the liquor mixed with the lemon juice, cream and pepper. Put the asparagus into the sauce to warm it up again over very low heat.

Goes well with: lean ham and parsley potatoes.

French Beans
△ ○

Approx. 85 calories per person

½ cup water
450g (16oz) deep-frozen
*   French beans*
1 tablespoon milk
1 tablespoon single cream
2 level teaspoons sugar
1 tablespoon butter or
*   margarine*
a pinch each of salt and
*   pepper*

Preparation time: 20 minutes.

Bring the water to the boil, put the frozen beans into it, cover and cook over low heat for 12 minutes. The beans done, drain them. Mix together the milk, cream, sugar and butter or margarine, add the beans, mix well and heat up once more over low heat. Season with salt and pepper to taste.

Goes well with: Fillet of Pork in Pastry (recipe on page 65) or stick of French bread.

Red or White Cabbage Salad (top); Radish Salad with Pear ▷ (front left); Raw Carrot Salad (bottom right); recipes on page 86

Vegetables and Salads

Red or White Cabbage Salad
△ ○ *

Approx. 165 calories per person

*1 head red or white cabbage
    (500g = 18oz)
1¼ teaspoons salt
2 apples
1 shallot
4 tablespoons oil
2 tablespoons wine vinegar
1 level tablespoon sugar
½ teaspoon caraway seeds*

Preparation time: 35 minutes.
Marinating time: 30 minutes.

Remove imperfect leaves from cabbage, quarter it, cut out the coarse stalk and shred fine. Mix the shredded cabbage with one teaspoon salt, cover with a plate or paper and put a weight on top; leave for 10 minutes. Peel the apples, removing core, and slice them thinly. Peel and dice shallot. Mix the oil, vinegar, sugar and caraway seeds with the remaining salt. Drain cabbage, mix it with the apples, shallots and salad dressing and let it infuse for 30 minutes.

Illustration on page 85

A hint: For white cabbage an improvement to the above recipe would be, if you took, instead of the apples, sliced celeriac and preserved red peppers.

Radish Salad with Pear
△ ○

Approx. 50 calories per person

*2 bunches radishes
1 pear
½ teaspoon salt
1 tablespoon oil
1 tablespoon wine vinegar
1 tablespoon chopped fresh
    chervil*

Preparation time: 15 minutes.

Clean, wash and slice radishes. Peel and quarter the pear, removing core and slice the quarters. Mix together the salt with oil and vinegar and add to the radishes and sliced pear. Sprinkle the chopped chervil over the salad before serving.

Illustration on page 85

Raw Carrot Salad
△ ○ *

Approx. 90 calories per person

*4 large carrots
1 apple
1 orange
1 lemon
2 level teaspoons sugar
4 tablespoons cream*

Preparation time: 20 minutes.

Scrape and wash the carrots. Peel and quarter the apple, removing core. Grate in turn 1 carrot and then one apple quarter in a vegetable mill, repeating the process with the remaining carrots and apple quarters. Squeeze out the orange and the lemon, mix the juice with the sugar and stir it into the grated mixture. Whisk the cream till semi-stiff and pour it over the salad just before serving.

Illustration on page 85

A tip: Deep-freeze without the cream.

Vegetables and Salads

Radish and Corn Salad

△ ○

Approx. 70 calories per person

2 bunches radishes
200g (7oz) corn salad
½ beaker yoghurt from skimmed milk
2 tablespoons tomato ketchup
½ teaspoon salt
½ teaspoon white pepper

Preparation time: 20 minutes.

Clean, rinse and slice radishes. Pick over the corn salad, wash and separate the leaves. Mix the sliced radishes and the corn salad leaves together in a salad bowl. Mix the yoghurt with the ketchup, salt and pepper and sprinkle the dressing over the salad.

Illustration below

Cucumber Salad

△ ○

Approx. 35 calories per person

1 fresh cucumber
3 tablespoons soya sauce
1 tablespoon oil
½ teaspoon salt
½ teaspoon coarsely ground pepper

Preparation time: 15 minutes.

Radish and Corn Salad (front)
◁ Cucumber Salad (back), recipes above

Vegetables and Salads

Wash the cucumber and cut it unpeeled into thin slices. Mix the soya sauce with the oil, salt and pepper and gently stir into the cucumber.

Illustration on page 87

Greek Salad
△ ○ ○

Approx. 150 calories per person

1 lettuce
1 onion
1 green or red pepper
15 stuffed olives
5 tomatoes
100g (3½oz) cheese made
*   from ewe's or goat's*
*   milk*
2 tablespoons oil
1 tablespoon wine vinegar
½ teaspoon salt
a pinch of dried basil

Preparation time: 20 minutes.

Separate the lettuce leaves, cut out the hard stalk, removing the imperfect leaves and tearing the very large leaves into smaller pieces. Wash the lettuce in cold water, drain and dry. Peel onion and cut into rings. Halve pepper, removing seeds, wash and cut into rings. Halve olives. Wash tomatoes and cut into eighths. Crumble the cheese into small pieces. Carefully mix in a salad bowl the

Greek Salad, recipe above

Vegetables and Salads

lettuce with the onion and pepper rings, olives, tomatoes and cheese. Stir together the oil, vinegar, salt and basil and pour the dressing over the salad.

Illustration on facing page

Salad Granada
△ ○

Approx. 105 calories per person

1 lettuce
2 small red shallots
4 tomatoes
15 stuffed olives
2 tablespoons oil
1 tablespoon wine vinegar
1 tablespoon brandy
1 level teaspoon salt
½ squashed garlic clove
a generous pinch of coarsely
*   ground pepper*

Preparation time: 15 minutes.

Separate lettuce leaves, removing imperfect ones and the stalk; tear the larger leaves into smaller pieces. Wash and dry lettuce. Peel shallots and cut into rings. Wash and dry tomatoes before cutting them into slices. Halve the olives. Mix the lettuce with the shallot rings, tomato slices and halves in a salad bowl. Stir together the oil with the vinegar, brandy, salt, squashed garlic and ground

Salad Granada, recipe above

Vegetables and Salads

pepper; pour dressing over the salad.

Illustration on page 89

Salad Niçoise
△ ○ ○

Approx. 260 calories per person

2 eggs
1 small lettuce
½ head of endive salad
4 tomatoes
100g (3½oz) tuna fish (canned)
12 anchovy fillets
10 black olives
10 green olives
1 can artichoke bottoms
1 onion
½ clove garlic
3 tablespoons olive oil
2 tablespoons wine vinegar
½ teaspoon salt
¼ teaspoon white pepper

Preparation time: 20 minutes.

Boil the eggs for ten minutes. Clean the lettuce and separate leaves, wash, dry and drain them. Cut the endive into strips, washing and drying these thoroughly.

Salad Niçoise, recipe above

Wash the tomatoes and cut them into eighths. Cut the tuna fish into even-sized pieces. Cut the anchovy fillets into strips. Halve the olives, removing the stones. Drain the artichokes and cut them into quarters. Peel the onion and cut it into rings; pour boiling water over them and drain. Peel garlic clove and cut very fine. Rinse the eggs under cold water, peel and cut them into eighths. Line a salad bowl with the lettuce leaves. Stir together the garlic with the oil, vinegar, salt and pepper. Carefully mix the endive strips, tomatoes, tuna fish pieces, anchovy strips, olive halves, artichokes bottoms, onion rings, and egg wedges with the salad dressing and put this on top of the lettuce leaves.

Illustration below

Goes well with: toast or wholemeal bread.

Brussels Sprouts Salad
△ ○ * *

Approx. 125 calories per person

500g (18oz) Brussels sprouts
1 cup hot water
½ teaspoon salt
½ cup wine vinegar
2 tablespoons oil
½ onion
¼ teaspoon pepper

Preparation time: 25 minutes.
Marinating time: 12 hours.

Remove the outer leaves of the sprouts, put the firm inner part with the hot water and salt into a saucepan, cover and cook over low heat for 20 minutes.

Vegetables and Salads

When the sprouts are done, pour the vegetable liquor into a bowl. Mix the liquor with the wine vinegar and oil. Peel the onion, cut it into small pieces and stir together with the pepper into the Brussels sprouts. Cover the bowl and let the salad marinate for at least 12 hours in the refrigerator.

A hint: The steamed Brussels sprouts, after being drained, may also be deep-frozen. In that case the vegetable liquor should be allowed to cool and then be deep-frozen separately. When wanted, the sprouts and the liquor are covered and allowed to thaw. They are then mixed with the vinegar, oil, onion and pepper and allowed to marinate for a further few hours.

Savoury Chicory Salad
△ ○

Approx. 70 calories per person

2 pieces of chicory (400g = 14oz)
2 tangerines
3 tablespoons yoghurt from skimmed milk
2 tablespoons cream

1 tablespoon lemon juice
a good pinch each of salt, pepper and sugar

Preparation time: 15 minutes.

Cut out from the chicory at the root end a wedge and remove imperfect leaves. Cut the chicory into thin slices, briefly rinse them under cold water and drain. Peel the tangerines and cut them into small pieces, removing any pips. Mix the yoghurt with the cream, lemon juice, salt, pepper and sugar and tangerine pieces and gently stir the dressing into the chicory. Serve at once.

Cucumber Salad with Cottage Cheese
△ ○

Approx. 80 calories per person

a few lettuce leaves in perfect condition
2 tablespoons wine vinegar
2 teaspoons sugar
½ teaspoon poppy seeds
150g (5½oz) cottage cheese
½ fresh cucumber

Preparation time: 20 minutes.

Wash and dry lettuce leaves. Bring to the boil the wine vinegar, sugar and poppy seeds and allow to cool. Line a salad bowl with the lettuce leaves and distribute the cottage cheese on them. Wash and dry the cucumber and cut it, unpeeled, into slices. Arrange the cucumber slices on top of the cottage cheese and pour the – by now cold – salad dressing over the cucumber slices.

Radish Salad
△ ○

Approx. 75 calories per person

4 bunches of radishes
½ onion
2 tomatoes
1 level teaspoon salt
a pinch each of garlic powder and pepper
1 teaspoon freshly chopped mint
1 teaspoon lemon juice
2 tablespoons oil
1 tablespoon parsley

Preparation time: 20 minutes.

91

Vegetables and Salads

Clean and wash radishes and cut them into slices. Peel and dice onion. Wash tomatoes and cut them into small pieces. Mix together the salt, garlic powder, pepper, mint, lemon juice and oil and stir the dressing under the salad; sprinkle it with parsley before serving.

Danish Salad

△ ○ ○

Approx. 295 calories per person

300g (11oz) deep-frozen mixture of peas and carrots
75g (2½oz) macaroni
1 level teaspoon salt
100g (3½oz) lean uncooked ham
150g (5½oz) canned asparagus tips
100g (3½oz) curd cheese from skimmed milk
1 level teaspoon sugar
1 tablespoon mayonnaise
½ beaker yoghurt from skimmed milk
4 tablespoons chopped mixed herbs
2 small tomatoes
1 small piece fresh cucumber

Preparation time: 35 minutes.
Time to cool: 20 minutes.

Put the deep-frozen vegetables into 3 tablespoons of salted boiling water, cover and steam for 6 minutes over low heat. Bring to the boil plenty of water with the salt, break the macaroni into roughly even-sized lengths and boil them in the water for 15 minutes. Cut the uncooked ham into fine strips. Drain the asparagus tips. Stir together curd cheese with the sugar, mayonnaise, yoghurt and finely chopped herbs. Wash tomatoes and cut them into eighths. Wash the cucumber and slice it unpeeled. The cooked vegetables are drained in a sieve and allowed to cool. The cooked macaroni is rinsed in cold water and likewise drained. Mix the vegetables with the macaroni, ham strips and asparagus tips, pour the curd cheese dressing over the salad, which is now placed in the refrigerator to marinate for 20 minutes. Before serving, garnish with tomato wedges and cucumber slices.

Illustration below

Goes well with: crackers or wholemeal biscuits.

Danish Salad, recipe above

Vegetables and Salads

Green Salad
△ ○

Approx. 25 calories per person

1 lettuce (approx. 200g = 7oz)
1 tablespoon oil
1 tablespoon wine vinegar
2 tablespoons single cream
a pinch each of salt and pepper
2 tablespoons finely chopped fresh herbs
a pinch of sugar (optional)

Preparation time: 10 minutes.

Separate the lettuce leaves, tear off imperfect pieces and remove hard stalk. The larger lettuce leaves should be torn into smaller pieces. Wash the salad in cold water and dry. Mix the oil with the vinegar, single cream, salt and pepper. Shortly before serving, gently stir the dressing into the salad as well as the freshly chopped herbs.

Possible Variations: You may want to add 2 tomatoes, cut into eighths, to the salad, in which case you must reckon 5 calories more per person. You could mix a finely sliced orange into it, increasing the calories by 15 per person, or add a bunch of finely sliced radishes, bringing the calories up by a further 4 per person. Another possible addition is a green pepper, cut into strips — making an additional 7 calories per person.

Apple and Sauerkraut Salad
△ ○

Approx. 140 calories per person

325g (12oz) canned sauerkraut
2 apples
2 pickled cucumbers
2 onions
a bunch of fresh mixed herbs (dill, parsley, chives, lemon balm etc.)
½ teaspoon salt
2 level tablespoons sugar
1–2 tablespoons lemon juice
2 tablespoons oil

Preparation time: 20 minutes.
Marinating time: 30 minutes.

Lift the sauerkraut out of the can, tease it with 2 forks and cut any larger pieces into smaller ones. Core the apples, cut them first into slices and then the slices into batons. Cut the pickled cucumbers likewise into batons. Peel and dice the onions, rinse the herbs under cold water, drain and chop them. Mix the apple and cucumber batons, the diced onions and the finely chopped herbs under the sauerkraut and season to taste with the sugar, salt and lemon juice. Heat the oil thoroughly in a frying-pan and pour it hot over the salad. Stir thoroughly once again and put it into a cool place to marinate for 30 minutes.

Goes well with: steaks and any kind of bread.

Potato Salad
△ ○

Approx. 155 calories per person

500g (18oz) potatoes
1 teaspoon caraway seeds
1 pickled cucumber
1 apple
½ cup preserved beetroot
1 onion
¼ cup boiling water
1 tablespoon oil

Vegetables and Salads

*a generous dash of wine
 vinegar*
*a pinch each of salt, pepper,
 sugar and marjoram*

Preparation time: 30 minutes.

Brush the potatoes thoroughly and steam them in a little boiling water, together with the caraway seeds, for 25 minutes over medium heat. The saucepan should be covered. Dice the pickled cucumber. Peel the apple, quarter it and remove core; slice the apple quarters. Cut beetroot into strips or dice, keeping the liquor. Peel and finely dice onion. Drain the cooked potatoes, refresh them under cold water before peeling and slicing them. The potatoes, while still warm, are now mixed with hot boiling water, oil, vinegar, salt, pepper, sugar and marjoram, finally adding the diced cucumber, apple slices, beetroot pieces and onion dice. Cover the salad and allow it to marinate for a few minutes at room temperature.

Bean and Carrot Salad
△ ○

Approx. 80 calories per person

4 tablespoons water
a pinch of salt
*600g (22oz) deep-frozen
 mixed French beans and
 carrots*
½ teaspoon mustard powder
½ teaspoon celery salt
1 level teaspoon flour
½ cup milk
1 egg yolk
3 tablespoons wine vinegar
*dietary sweetener equivalent
 to 1 teaspoon sugar*

Preparation time: 20 minutes.

Bring the water with the salt to the boil, put the deep-frozen vegetables into it, cover the saucepan and steam for 10 minutes over low heat. The cooked vegetables are drained through a sieve and allowed to cool. Mix the mustard powder with the celery salt and flour and stir the cold milk into the mixture. The milk with its ingredients is now brought to the boil several times while being constantly stirred. Remove from heat and stir the egg yolk, wine vinegar and sweetener into it. Mix the by now cool vegetables with the salad dressing.

Melon Salad
△ *

Approx. 65 calories per person

2 large, ripe tomatoes
¼ water melon
1 small lettuce
2 tablespoons oil
*1 tablespoon freshly
 squeezed lemon juice*
¼ teaspoon Worcester sauce
½ teaspoon salt
a good pinch of pepper
½ teaspoon sugar

Preparation time: 20 minutes.

Bring about ¼ litre (½ pt) water to the boil. Make a few incisions at the bottom end of the tomatoes, pour the boiling water over them, and leave them in it for a few minutes. With a special cutter or a teaspoon cut balls from the inner part of the melon. Peel the tomatoes and cut them into eighths. Remove the imperfect leaves from the lettuce, cut out the hard stalk, break up the lettuce leaves, wash them in cold water, drain and dry them. Stir together the oil, lemon juice, Worcester sauce, salt, pepper and sugar. Mix all the salad ingredients and sprinkle the dressing over them.

Vegetables and Salads

Piquant Apple Salad

△ ○

Approx. 80 calories per person

1 carrot
2 apples
1 teaspoon lemon juice
½ teaspoon sugar
1 cup preserved celeriac
½ beaker yoghurt from
*   skimmed milk*
3 tablespoons single cream
¼ teaspoon salt
a pinch each of pepper and
*   paprika*

Preparation time: 20 minutes.

Clean, wash and scrape the carrot. Peel the apples, remove core and cut them first into slices and then into batons. Sprinkle the lemon juice and the sugar over the apple pieces. Drain the celeriac and, if not already in strips, cut likewise into batons. Grate the carrot and mix it with the apple and celery batons. Stir together the yoghurt, cream, salt, pepper and paprika and pour the dressing over the salad.

Illustration on page 107

Hamburg Cucumber Salad

△ ○

Approx. 35 calories per person

1 small fresh cucumber
the juice of ½ lemon
4 tablespoons yoghurt from
*   skimmed milk*
a generous pinch of salt
1–1½ teaspoons sugar

Preparation time: 15 minutes.

Peel the cucumber only if the peel is hard; otherwise wash it unpeeled before slicing it on the mandoline. Stir together the lemon juice with the yoghurt, salt and sugar and add this mixture to the cucumber slices.

American Cucumber Salad

△ ○

Approx. 25 calories per person

1 fresh cucumber
1 beaker yoghurt from
*   skimmed milk*
2 tablespoons finely
*   chopped dill*
½ teaspoon salt
a pinch of white pepper
a pinch of sugar

Preparation time: 15 minutes.

Peel the cucumber only if the skin is hard; otherwise wash it unpeeled before grating it in the vegetable mill. Mix the cucumber with the yoghurt, dill, salt, pepper and sugar.

Soufflés and Casseroles

Fish Stew
△ ○ ○

Approx. 185 calories per person

2 onions
1 large head of fish
1 bay leaf
1 level teaspoon salt
¼ teaspoon pepper
1 litre (almost 2pt) water
4 medium-sized potatoes
500g (18oz) tomatoes
500g (18oz) haddock
1 tablespoon oil
a pinch of garlic powder
2 tablespoons finely
    chopped parsley
a few small capers
5 stuffed olives

Preparation time: 50 minutes.

The onions are peeled and
one of them cut into eighths.
Put the fish head with the
bay leaf, onion eighths, salt
and pepper and water into a
saucepan, cover and cook
over low heat for 30 min-
utes. Peel, wash and dice the
potatoes. Make a few
incisions at the bottom end
of the tomatoes, pour
boiling water over them,
leave them in the water for
a few minutes and then
peel them. The second
onion is diced. The haddock
is washed, dabbed dry and
cut into even-sized dice.

Sieve the fish liquor and
cook the diced potatoes in
it over low heat for 20
minutes with the lid on.
Cut the peeled tomatoes
into eighths and add them
to the potatoes. Heat the
oil and lightly fry first the
diced onion and then the
diced haddock in it, stirring
all the time. Sprinkle with
the garlic powder. The
diced fish and onion are
now added to the potatoes
and tomatoes as well as the
parsley and the capers. Cut
the olives into fine slices and
add them to the fish stew,
which is now covered and
once again heated up over
very low heat.

Illustration on facing page

*Recommended second
course:* Garnished Fruit
Jellies (recipe on page 106)
or Delicate Strawberry
Snow (recipe on page 108).

Minced Beef Goulash
△ ○ ○ *

Approx. 225 calories per person

500g (18oz) white cabbage
2 peppers
1 onion
4 medium-sized potatoes
1 tablespoon oil
400g (14oz) minced beef
2 cups hot water
½ teaspoon salt
a pinch each of pepper,
    garlic powder and paprika

Preparation time: 20 minutes.
Cooking time: 20 minutes.

Remove any imperfect outer
leaves of the cabbage as well
as the coarse stalks before
slicing the cabbage finely.
Halve the peppers, remove
seeds and cut them into
strips. Peel and dice onions.
Peel and wash the potatoes
and cut them into cubes.
Heat the oil in a rather large
saucepan and in it lightly
fry the diced onion and the
minced beef, stirring
constantly. Add the cabbage
and pepper strips and lightly
fry them also. Mix into it
the water, salt, pepper,
garlic powder and paprika.
Finally add the potato
cubes, then cover and cook
for 20 minutes over low
heat.

Fish Stew, recipe on this page ▷

Soufflés and Casseroles

Recommended second course: Delicate Strawberry Snow (recipe on page 108) or Orange Julienne (recipe on page 108).

Swiss Eggs au Gratin

△ *

Approx. 365 calories per person

200g (7oz) Emmental cheese
1 tablespoon butter or margarine
4 tablespoons cottage cheese
1 tablespoon mustard
½ teaspoon salt
a generous pinch of cayenne pepper
½ cup water
6 eggs

Preparation time: 15 minutes.
Cooking time: 25 minutes.

Preheat the oven to 180°C (375°F; gas mark 5). Thinly slice the Emmental cheese. Grease an ovenproof dish with half the butter or margarine and place the cheese slices into it. Whisk together the cottage cheese with the mustard, salt, cayenne pepper and the water and spread half of the mixture on the Emmental. Whisk the eggs and pour them over the cottage cheese in the oven-proof dish. Now put the remainder of the butter on top of that. Cook for 25 minutes in the oven until the top is golden brown.

Goes well with: Sticks of French bread and tomato salad.
Suggested second course: Mixed Fruit Dessert (recipe on page 106).

Kohl-rabi and Beef Casserole

△ ○ ○

Approx. 275 calories per person

4 medium-sized kohl-rabi
8 small potatoes
2 medium-sized carrots
400g (14oz) brisket of beef
1 tablespoon oil
1 cup hot water
½ teaspoon salt
¼ teaspoon pepper
a good pinch of grated nutmeg
2 tablespoons chopped parsley

Preparation time: 20 minutes.

Cooking time: 40 minutes.

The kohl-rabi are washed, thinly peeled, any woody pieces are removed before they're cut into thin slices. The tender stalks of the kohl-rabi greens are washed, drained, cut finely, covered and kept. Brush the potatoes under cold running water, peel and dice them. Grate the carrots, wash and slice them. Briefly rinse the brisket under cold water, dab dry and cut into even-sized slices. Now heat the oil in a shallow stewing pan and briefly fry the beef slices on both sides over fierce heat. Add the kohl-rabi, potatoes and carrots to the meat as well as the hot water, sprinkling the salt, pepper and nutmeg over the stew. Stir everything once again, cover and cook over medium heat for 40 minutes. Before serving, garnish with the chopped parsley and the kohl-rabi greens.

Recommended second course: Refreshing Buttermilk Dessert (recipe on page 108) or Mandarin Yoghurt (recipe on page 108).

Soufflés and Casseroles

Leek Casserole – Farmer's Fashion
△ ○ ○

Approx. 385 calories per person

500g (18oz) leeks
8 small potatoes
50g (2oz) streaky bacon
1 cup water
a pinch each of salt and
*   pepper*
300g (11oz) boiling sausage

Preparation time: 15 minutes.
Cooking time: 35 minutes.

The leeks are cleaned, halved lengthways, thoroughly washed under cold running water and cut into small slices. The potatoes are peeled, washed and diced. The streaky bacon is likewise diced. Bring the water with the salt and pepper to the boil, the leeks, bacon and diced potatoes are put into the boiling water, covered and cooked for 5 minutes; reduce heat and let simmer over very low heat for a further 30 minutes. Cut the sausage into even-sized cubes, add to the stew, stir everything well together, cover and warm up once again.

Suggested dessert: Coffee Mousse (recipe on page 110).

Delicate Vegetable Souffle
△ ○

Approx. 240 calories per person

100g (3½oz) boiled rice
300g (11oz) deep-frozen
*   peas*
280g (10oz) canned aspara-
*   gus*
2 tomatoes
100 to 115g (3½–4oz)
*   canned mushrooms*
2 eggs
50g (2oz) grated Gouda
*   cheese*

Preparation time: 25 minutes.

Preheat oven to maximum temperature. Spread the boiled rice on the bottom of an oven-proof dish. Distribute the deep-frozen peas over the rice and the asparagus with its liquid from the can on top of these. Wash the tomatoes, cut them into eighths and layer them on the asparagus. Drain the mushrooms and put them over the tomatoes. Whisk the eggs, stir the grated cheese into them and pour the mixture over the vegetables and bake in the oven for 25 minutes.

Goes well with: escalope of veal nature or Fillet of Pork in Pastry (recipe on page 65).
Suitable dessert: Fruit Yoghurt (recipe on page 109).

Ghanaen Fish Ragoût
△ ○ ○

Approx. 220 calories per person

500g (18oz) filleted bream
½ teaspoon salt
½ teaspoon cayenne pepper
4 tomatoes
4 onions
2 aubergines
1 orange
1 tablespoon olive oil
10 stuffed olives
1 cup instant meat stock

Preparation time: 25 minutes.
Cooking time: 25 minutes.

Rinse the fish, dab it dry before cutting it into even-sized cubes. Sprinkle with salt and cayenne pepper. Wash the tomatoes and quarter them. Peel the onions and cut them into rings. Peel the aubergines, halve them, removing the seeds, and slice the halves. Peel and dice the orange.

Soufflés and Casseroles

Heat the oil in a rather large saucepan and lightly fry the onions in it, add also the aubergines and the diced fish to fry briefly; mix the tomato quarters, diced orange, olives and meat stock with the fish, cover and stew for a further 20 minutes.

Illustration below

Goes well with: boiled rice or French bread.
Recommended Dessert: California Beaker (recipe on page 110).

Spinach Soufflé
△ ○ ○

Approx. 270 calories per person

750g (27oz) fresh spinach
2 cups water
1 level teaspoon salt
1 onion
200g (7oz) very lean boiled ham
1 tablespoon oil
1 cup boiled rice
1 egg
a pinch each of pepper and grated nutmeg

1 tablespoon butter in flakes
1 tomato

Preparation time: 40 minutes.
Cooking time: 20 minutes.

Pick over the spinach and wash thoroughly. Bring the 2 cups of water together with the salt to the boil, add the spinach, cover and steam for a few minutes until the spinach collapses. Peel and dice the onion. Dice the ham as well. Drain the spinach and cut it coarsely. Heat the oil in a

Ghanaen Fish Ragoût, recipe on page 99
Spinach 'Kaltschale', recipe on page 23; Spinach Soufflé, ▷
recipe on this page

Soufflés and Casseroles

fireproof dish and fry the diced onion lightly in it. Preheat oven to a temperature of 220°C (425°F; gas mark 7). Spread half the spinach over the diced onion, putting on top first the diced ham and then the remaining spinach. Mix the rice with the egg yolk, pepper and grated nutmeg. The egg white is whisked till stiff and folded under the rice. The rice mixture is now placed as the final layer onto the soufflé with the flaked butter on top. Bake for about 20 minutes.

To serve: Garnish the soufflé with tomato slices.

Illustration on page 101

Recommended Desserts: Refreshing Buttermilk Dessert (recipe on page 108) or Apple Curd Cheese Marianne (recipe on page 110).

Beef and Rice Casserole △ ○ * *

Approx. 275 calories per person

1 onion
400g (14oz) best chuck steak
1 tablespoon oil
100g (3½oz) rice
1½ cups water
½ teaspoon salt
¼ teaspoon white pepper
2 tomatoes
1 carrot
¼ teaspoon instant meat concentrate

Preparation time: 10 minutes.
Cooking time: 20 minutes.

Peel and dice the onion. Briefly rinse the meat under cold water, removing skin and sinews, and cut into small even-sized cubes. Heat the oil in a shallow saucepan and in it fry the diced onion and beef for about 5 minutes, stirring constantly. Add the rice and lightly fry it as well; fill up with the water, salt and pepper, cover and cook for 20 minutes over low heat. Wash and dice the tomatoes; scrape, wash and grate the carrot. 5 minutes before the meat is done, add the tomato pieces and the grated carrot to it. Finally, stir in the meat concentrate.

Goes well with: American Cucumber Salad (recipe on page 95) or Radish Salad (recipe on page 91). *Suitable dessert:* Stuffed Pineapple (recipe page 111).

Lamb and Vegetable Casserole △ ○ ○

Approx. 390 calories per person

500 grams (18oz) loin of lamb
1 onion
1 tablespoon oil
1 tablespoon tomato purée
1 level tablespoon flour
1 level teaspoon salt
¼ teaspoon pepper
¼ packet dried soup vegetables
1 carrot
3 tomatoes
8 medium-sized potatoes
10 pickled silver onions
100g (3½oz) deep-frozen peas
100g (3½oz) deep-frozen French beans
1 teaspoon chopped fresh basil

Preparation time: 1 hour.

Soufflés and Casseroles

Briefly rinse the meat under cold water, remove skins and sinews and cut into cubes of even size. Peel and dice the onion. Heat the oil in a rather large casserole, lightly fry the diced onion and meat cubes, stirring constantly; add the tomato purée, sprinkle with the flour and lightly fry as well, turning all the while. Add the salt, pepper and soup vegetables, and pour enough hot water over the meat to cover it. Put the lid on and braise for 40 minutes over medium heat. Scrape and wash the carrot before cutting it into batons. Make a few incisions in the bottom end of the tomatoes, pour some boiling water over them and let them lie in the water for a few minutes before peeling and cutting them into eighths. Peel, wash and dice the potatoes. 20 minutes before the meat is done, add the diced potatoes, tomato eighths, carrot batons, silver onions and deep-frozen peas and beans, cover and continue the braising process for another 20 to 25 minutes (you may possibly have to add a little hot water). Sprinkle with chopped basil before serving.

Illustration below

Suitable Dessert: Mixed Fruit Dessert (recipe on page 106).

Lamb and Vegetable Casserole, recipe above

103

Soufflés and Casseroles

Chicken and Vegetable Casserole
△ ○ ○ ＊ ＊

Approx. 495 calories per person

2 onions
1 roasting chicken weighing
*   1 kilogram (2¼lb)*
2 tablespoons oil
½ litre (1pt) instant chicken
*   stock*
½ teaspoon salt
¼ teaspoon pepper
½ teaspoon curry powder
1 red pepper
1 green pepper
500g (18oz) tomatoes
250g (9oz) French beans
1 salad cucumber
100g (3½oz) fresh mush-
*   rooms*
a pinch of garlic powder
2 tablespoons finely
*   chopped parsley*

Preparation time: 20 minutes.
Cooking time: 40 minutes.

Peel and dice the onions.
Wash the chicken inside and
out, and carve it into 8
pieces. Heat the oil in a
rather large stewing pan.
Stir the onions into the fat
and lightly brown them;
lightly fry also the chicken
portions on all sides, add
salt, pepper, curry powder
and chicken stock, cover
and cook for 30 minutes
over low heat. Halve the
peppers, removing seeds,
wash the pepper halves and
cut them into strips. Wash
the tomatoes and cut them
into eighths. String the
beans, wash them and cut
the larger ones into
smaller pieces. Wash, peel
and dice the cucumber.
Clean the mushrooms
thoroughly and halve the
larger ones. When the
chicken has cooked for
20 minutes, add the vege-
tables to it, cover and cook
over low heat for a further
20 minutes. Before serving,
add some garlic powder to
taste and sprinkle the
parsley over it.

Illustration on facing page

Goes well with: French
bread.
Recommended Dessert:
Coffee Mousse (recipe on
page 110).

Desserts

Mixed Fruit Dessert
△ ○

Approx. 90 calories per person

1 banana
1 apple
2 teaspoons lemon juice
1 level teaspoon sugar
1 orange
10 cocktail cherries

Preparation time: 15 minutes.

Peel the banana and cut into slices. Cut the apple, unpeeled, into wedges and the wedges into small slices. Sprinkle the lemon juice and the sugar over the banana slices and the apple pieces. Peel the orange, divide into wedges, cut the wedges into pieces, removing the pips. Halve the cocktail cherries or quarter them and mix them with the orange pieces under the other ingredients. Put the fruit salad in a glass and let it macerate for a short time before serving.

Illustration on facing page

Raspberries in White Wine Jelly
△ ○ ○

Approx. 65 calories per person

the juice of one lemon
¼ litre (½pt) water
1 small packet ground gelatine
dietary sweetener equivalent to two tablespoons sugar
¼ litre (½pt) white wine
200g (7oz) fresh or unsugared deep-frozen raspberries

Preparation time: 20 minutes.
Cooling time: 3–4 hours.

Add enough water to the lemon juice to make ¼ litre (½pt) liquid. Soak the gelatine in 5 tablespoons of the lemon and water mixture for 10 minutes. Heat up the remaining lemon water, dissolve the dietary sweetener in it and then stir in the gelatine until it's dissolved. Remove the liquid from the fire and add the white wine, stirring constantly. When the jelly is beginning to set fill 4 individual bowls or sundae glasses one quarter full and put them in the refrigerator to set completely. Distribute the raspberries into the glasses, fill up with the remaining jelly and return to the refrigerator until the jelly is completely firm.

Garnished Fruit Jellies
△ ○

Approx. 90 calories per person

½ litre (1pt) redcurrant juice
6 leaves white gelatine
the juice of ½ lemon
1 level tablespoon sugar
100g (3½oz) curd cheese from skimmed milk
2 tablespoons single cream
1 small packet vanilla sugar

Preparation time: 20 minutes.
Cooling time: 3–4 hours.

Soak the gelatine in half the redcurrant juice and dissolve it over low heat by stirring it for 15 minutes. Add the remaining redcurrant juice as well as the lemon juice and the sugar, stir and let it get cool. As the liquid begins to set, fill it into 4 sundae glasses and let it get completely firm in the refrigerator. Stir together the curd cheese and single cream as well as the vanilla sugar and garnish the jellies with this mixture.

Apple Salad (top), recipe on page 95
Mixed Fruit Dessert (bottom), recipe on this page ▷

Desserts

Buttermilk Dessert
△○

Approx. 70 calories per person

*1 small packet of ground
   gelatine
5 tablespoons water
dietary sweetener (equalling
   1 tablespoon sugar)
½ litre (1pt) buttermilk
2 egg whites
2 tablespoons raspberry
   syrup
1 tablespoon blackberry
   liqueur*

Preparation time: 15 minutes.
Cooling time: 3–4 hours.

Soak the gelatine in cold
water for 10 minutes; the
soaked gelatine is then dissolved in a bain-marie, together with the dietary
sweetener (stir constantly).
It is then whisked together
with the buttermilk until
the latter begins to set.
Beat the egg whites till stiff
and fold them under the
dessert, before it's completely set. Fill the sweet into
4 sundae glasses and put
these into the refrigerator
to become completely firm.
Mix the raspberry syrup
with the blackberry liqueur
and pour over each portion
before serving.

Orange Salad Julienne
△○

Approx. 70 calories per person

*2 oranges
1 level tablespoon sugar
4 tablespoons single cream
4 tablespoons corn flakes*

Preparation time: 15 minutes.

Wash one of the oranges in
hot water; remove about
one third of the skin
without the pith and cut
into very fine julienne
strips. Now peel both
oranges and cut them, first
into thin slices and thereafter into eighths. Arrange
these small orange slices on
4 dessert plates. Mix thoroughly the sugar with the
cream and pour over the
fruit. Sprinkle the corn
flakes and the orange
julienne over the 4 portions.

Mandarin Yoghurt
△○

Approx. 65 calories per person

*the juice of 1 lemon
dietary sweetener (equalling
   1 tablespoon sugar)
3 mandarins
2 beakers yoghurt from
   skimmed milk
1 small packet vanilla sugar*

Preparation time: 10 minutes.

Dissolve the dietary sweetener in the lemon juice. Peel
the mandarins, separate
them into wedges and cut
these into small pieces. Stir
the yoghurt together with
the lemon juice and vanilla
sugar and fold the mandarin
pieces under.

Strawberry Mousse
△○○

Approx. 70 calories per person

*400g (14oz) fresh straw-
   berries
dietary sweetener (equalling
   1 tablespoon sugar)
2 tablespoons single cream
2 egg whites*

Desserts

Preparation time: 15 minutes.

Wash, clean and halve strawberries. Dissolve the sweetener in the cream. Whisk egg whites till stiff. Squash the strawberries with a fork. Mix the sweetened cream into them and fold egg whites under the fruit mousse. Fill into 4 individual bowls and serve at once.

Fruit Yoghurt
△ ○

Approx. 125 calories per person

2 apples
1 pear
1 banana
1 orange
the juice of 1 lemon
2 level tablespoons sugar
1 beaker yoghurt from
  skimmed milk

Preparation time: 15 minutes.

Peel all fruit, removing cores from apples and pears. Cut the fruit into slices and mix in a bowl. Stir together the lemon juice, sugar and yoghurt, gently mix with the fruit, cover to macerate for a few minutes.

Illustration below

Fruit Yoghurt, recipe above

Desserts

Apple Curd Cheese Marianne
△ ○

Approx. 80 calories per person

2 apples
200g (7oz) curd cheese
*   from skimmed milk*
2 teaspoons honey
1 teaspoon lemon juice

Preparation time: 20 minutes.

The apples are peeled, quartered, cored and then grated. When grated, mix them with the curd cheese, honey and lemon juice. Should the apples produce too little juice and should the curd cheese therefore be too dry, you may have to add a little water.

California Beaker
△ ○ ○

Approx. 165 calories per person

400g (14oz) strawberries,
*   fresh; or deep-frozen,*
*   unsugared strawberries*
2 oranges
dietary sweetener equalling
*   1 tablespoon of sugar*
2 tubs (400g = 14oz)
*   cottage cheese*

Preparation time: 20 minutes.

The strawberries, if of the fresh variety, are washed several times in cold water, picked over and quartered; the deep-frozen variety are allowed to thaw. Squeeze the oranges and dissolve the dietary sweetener in the juice. Stir together the orange juice and cottage cheese, fill into four individual bowls, placing the strawberries on top.

Illustration below

California Beaker,
recipe above

110

Desserts

Coffee Mousse
△△○○

Approx. 40 calories per person

*1 small packet of ground
   gelatine
1 cup cold water
1 cup milk
1 level tablespoon instant
   coffee
a pinch of salt
dietary sweetener equivalent
   to 1 teaspoon of sugar
2 level teaspoons vanilla
   sugar
2 egg whites*

Preparation time: 15 minutes.
Cooling time: 3–4 hours.

Soak the gelatine in the cold water for 10 minutes, then dissolve it in a bain-marie, stirring constantly. Add the milk, instant coffee, salt, sweetener and vanilla sugar to the dissolved gelatine, leaving the mixture for a further few minutes in the bain-marie, and go on stirring until everything is well dissolved and mixed thoroughly. Now remove the coffee mousse from the bain-marie, and continue stirring until the mousse begins to set. Whisk the egg whites till stiff and fold them under the mousse which is then filled into four individual bowls; these are placed in the refrigerator to set completely.

Stuffed Pineapple
△△○○

Approx. 250 calories per person

*1 fresh pineapple
1 can mandarin segments
1 glass jar cocktail cherries
1 cup preserved goose-
   berries
½ cup canned apricot halves
2 tablespoons pistachio nuts
2 tablespoons peeled pine
   kernels
1 liqueur glass Grand
   Marnier
1 liqueur glass pear brandy*

Preparation time: 25 minutes.

Cut off one third of the *length* of the pineapple (see illustration) and hollow out the fruit completely. Cut the flesh into small cubes. Drain the mandarin segments, cocktail cherries, gooseberries and apricots, collecting the juice (you may like to cut the fruit into slightly smaller pieces). Mix all the fruit with the pineapple cubes, pistachio nuts and pine kernels and fill the mixture into the larger part of the hollowed-out pineapple. Stir together one cup of the mixed fruit juice with the Grand Marnier and pear brandy, pour the mixture over the fruit and allow to macerate for a short while.

Illustration on page 112

Keeping slim

If you prepare your meals for several weeks in accordance with the recipes in the preceding pages, you can be sure of losing several pounds. Maybe you'll then want to reduce your weight still further or, perhaps, content with the success achieved, you'll wish only to keep your weight at the new level. In either case it's important to stick to the rules you've become accustomed to and, above all, to remain conscious of your daily calorie allowance. Let's consider a woman 5' 5" tall weighing 150lb — 28lb 10oz in excess of her ideal weight. To lose these pounds, her daily calorie intake would need reducing to 1,500, the remainder of her energy requirements being supplied by her body's fat reserves. Such a drastic diet couldn't be kept up indefinitely, of course, for sooner or later the available fat reserves would be exhausted; any further slimming would almost certainly have serious consequences for her health. This, then, is the time for a little discretion. For a period of 2—3 weeks she should increase her daily allowance to 1,800 calories which — provided there's no change in her way of life — should enable her to maintain her ideal weight. If

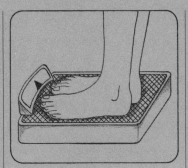

Always weigh yourself in the morning, before breakfast and before dressing

she's successful in this, she can increase her daily allowance over the following few weeks to 2,000 and, subsequently, to 2,200, 2,400 or even 2,600 calories. The moment the scales begin to show the slightest rise, however, she must stop increasing her calorie intake, her true calorie needs having now been established. Finally, remember always to weigh yourself in the morning, before breakfast and before dressing.

Don't cheat with the side dishes

To slim and stay slim, it's important not to cheat — never interpret the 'approximate' in your favour — and if in doubt, eat less rather than more.
In the following list you'll find the side dishes recommended in the recipe section, plus a few others; included is the calorie value per person, for probably not every member of the family will be subject to the same strict diet.

Bread and Bakery Products

1 cracker, about 8
Crispbread (1 slice = 10g), about 38
French bread (1 slice = 40g), about 111
Ordinary bread (1 slice = 40g), about 100
Pumpernickel (1 slice = 40g), about 97
1 roll (50g), about 140
Toasted white bread (1 slice = 30g), about 75
Wholemeal bread (1 slice = 45g), about 105

Potatoes in Purée and Processed Form

Boiled potatoes, 2 medium-sized, about 57

◁ Stuffed Pineapple, recipe on page 111

113

Keeping slim

Dumplings made of raw potatoes, from a 220g packet containing 8 dumplings, per dumpling about 100

Dumplings made of an equal quantity of cooked and raw potatoes, from a 220g packet containing 8 dumplings, per dumpling about 94

Mashed potatoes, from a 125g packet for four people, with ½ litre water and ¼ litre milk, one portion about 115

Parsley potatoes, 2 medium-sized, with some parsley and ½ teaspoon butter, about 77

Potatoes in their jackets, 2 medium-sized, about 57

Rice and Pasta

Pasta, cooked in salt water, 50g uncooked, about 180

Rice, cooked in salt water, 50g uncooked, about 194

Deep-Frozen Vegetables

Brussels sprouts, cooked in salt water, 100g, about 42

Carrots, cooked in salt water, 100g, about 30

French beans, cooked in salt water, 100g, about 25

Kohl-rabi, cooked in salt water, 100g, about 26

Peas, cooked in salt water, 100g, about 32

Red cabbage, cooked in salt water, 100g, about 21

Red cabbage, cooked with 1 apple and 1 tablespoon fat, about 63

Spinach, cooked in salt water, 100g, about 20

Salads Preserved in Jars

Bean salad, 50g, about 45

Beetroot salad, 110g, about 55

Carrot salad, 50g, about 45

Celeriac salad, 50g, about 45

Pickled cucumber, 1 piece, 40g, about 16

Meat

Beef, boiled, 100g, about 260

Beef fillet, fried without fat or grilled, 200g, about 252

Beef rumpsteak, fried without fat or grilled, 200g, about 594

Beef steak, fried without fat or grilled, 200g, about 506

Beef Tatar, raw, 150g, about 110

Calf's liver, fried in 1 teaspoon oil, 100g, about 171

Frankfurt sausages, 1 pair, 100g, about 250

Ham, cooked, lean, 100g, about 274

Ham, uncooked, lean, 100g, about 344

Lamb Chops, fried without fat or grilled, 100g, about 370

Pork Cutlets, fried without fat or grilled, 100g, about 358

Pork Escalope, fried without fat or grilled, 150g, about 352

Pork Fillet, fried without fat or grilled, 150g, about 264

Veal cutlets nature, fried without fat or grilled, 100g, about 125

Veal, escalope nature, fried without fat or grilled, 150g, about 162

Veal, escalope nature, fried in 1 teaspoon oil, 150g, about 190

Vienna sausages, 1 pair, 100g, about 265

Keeping slim

Some suggestions for snacks

120 calories

- 1 beaker yoghurt from skimmed milk and 1 slice crispbread with 2 tomatoes, seasoned with salt and pepper and garnished with chives.
- 1 beaker fruit yoghurt and 1 butter biscuit.
- 1 slice crispbread with 1 tablespoon curd cheese from skimmed milk, seasoned with salt and pepper and sprinkled with parsley and with it 1 bunch radishes.
- 50g prawns with 1 tablespoon yoghurt from skimmed milk, 1 teaspoon tomato ketchup and seasoned with some herbs with one slice starch-reduced toast.
- 2 rusks, spread with 1 teaspoon butter.
- 1 grated apple, mixed with 1 teaspoon honey and 2 tablespoons curd cheese from skimmed milk.
- 3 apricots or 1 peach with 1 rusk.

150 calories

- ½ roll with 80g herrings in aspic.
- ½ roll with 50g corned beef and 2 slices pickled cucumber.

- 1 beaker buttermilk 1 slice crispbread with almost a teaspoon butter and 1 tomato.
- 1 slice wholemeal bread (45g) with 25g Limburg cheese (20% fat content).
- 1 cup instant meat broth with 1 egg yolk sprinkled with chopped chives and 1 slice crispbread with almost a teaspoon butter.
- 2 tomatoes and 1 slice rye bread (40g) with 1 tablespoon curd cheese from skimmed milk, mixed with anchovy paste.
- ⅛ litre orange juice and 1 slice starch-reduced toast with 1 tablespoon curd cheese from skimmed milk, mixed with herbs.
- 100g grapes and 2 rusks.

180 calories

- 20g Mortadella on 1 slice crispbread with 1 teaspoon butter, and 2 tomatoes.
- 50g Vienna sausages in slices, with 1 diced pickled cucumber mixed with 1 teaspoon tomato ketchup and 1 tablespoon curd cheese from skimmed milk.
- 50g Edam cheese (30% fat content) with one slice crispbread and 1 tomato.
- 1 beaker fruit yoghurt from skimmed milk and 2 rusks.
- 50g cooked cheese and 1 slice crispbread.

- ⅛ litre grapefruit juice and 1 slice wholemeal bread (45g) with almost 1 teaspoon butter.
- ½ roll and 50g prawns dressed with 2 tablespoons seasoned curd cheese from skimmed milk.
- ⅛ litre milk, 2 rusks and one mandarin.
- 1 hardboiled egg and one slice starch-reduced toast with almost a teaspoon butter.

Keeping slim

Measuring correctly, weighing correctly

Measuring and weighing are of the utmost importance to mini-calorie cooking. In the recipes in this book, quantities are given usually in spoons or cups, the main exceptions being those ingredients purchased by weight, such as deep-frozen food, meat, fish, vegetables, fruit and packaged items. Except for ready-packaged products where you know the weight, be careful to insist on the precise weight being given. Withstand the temptation of accepting from the retailer a 'little more' than you asked for, and keep a careful watch on his scales while he's serving you.

The success of your mini-calorie diet largely depends on accuracy; mere 'guestimates' just won't do — the difference between 70 and 80g (approximately 2½ and 3oz) of rice is already 36.8 calories! Inaccuracies like this, frequently repeated, can be the difference between success and failure. Kitchen scales accurate to a gram/ounce are a useful acquisition. With the aid of your scales, select a tea-spoon and a tablespoon which hold the exact quantities of the various

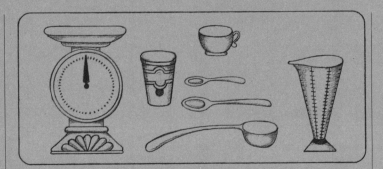

The success of a mini-calorie diet largely depends on the use of reliable and accurate weighing and measuring instruments (use the measuring beaker only for liquids).

ingredients, as given in the following table (that a level spoon *means* a level spoon and not a heaped one, need hardly be stressed). In-gredients given in grams should always be carefully weighed, but not with the measuring beaker, which isn't sufficiently accurate. American sets of measuring cups and spoons, now becoming available outside of the States, are very useful aids to accurate measurement.

Litre and Kilogram (Water)

1 litre (l) = 10 decilitres (dl)
= 100 centilitres (cl) =
1 kilogram (kg) =
1000 grams (g)
1 decilitre (dl) = 10 centilitres (cl) = 100 grams (g)
1 centilitre (cl) =
10 grams (g)
¼ l = 16 tablespoons =
approx. 1 soup plate
⅛ l = 8 tablespoons =
approx. 1 bare cup or glass
1/16 l = 4 tablespoons
2 cl = 1 liqueur glass

Keeping slim

Teaspoon, Tablespoon and Cup (in grams)

		1 level teaspoon	*1 level tablespoon*	*1 cup*
Baking powder	about	3	—	—
Butter		5	15	—
Semolina		4	12	100
Porridge oats			8	70
Honey		10	30	—
Cheese, grated		3	10	80
Cocoa		2	6	—
Marmalade, jelly, jam			25	—
Mayonnaise		10	30	240
Flour		3	10	80
Horseradish, grated		5	15	—
Nuts, grated		6	20	150
Oil		3	9	75
Icing sugar		3	10	—
Rice		5	15	120
Salt		5	15	—
Breadcrumbs		3	10	80
Cornflour		5	15	120
Water, milk		5	15	—
Cube sugar, 1 piece		3—5	9—15	—
Sugar		5	15	120

Rice as side dish 30g
Rice as main dish 50g
Rice as soup garnish 10g
Sauce served separately $1/16$ l
Soup as first course $1/8$ l
Soup as main dish $1/4$ l
Vegetables as side dish
  150—200g
Vegetables as main course
  250—400g

What quantities should you serve?

The following specifications apply only to mini-calorie cooking. You should reckon per person:
Cheese as dessert 10—30g
Fish with bones 250g
Fish without bones 200g
Fruit as dessert 100—150g
Meat, boned 120—180g
Meat with bones 180—250g
Mussels 300—500g
Other desserts 50g
Oysters 6—12g
Pasta as main dish 50g
Pasta as a soup garnish 15g
Pasta as side dish 30g
Potatoes as side dish 85g
  (3 small potatoes)
Potatoes as main course 100g
  (4 small potatoes)
Poultry with bones 200g
Poultry without bones 150g
Pulses as main dish 50g

Keeping slim

Calorie Table

The following calorie table is no more than a selection from the almost infinite variety of the foodstuffs on offer. The food values given frequently differ slightly from one another with the result that data is approximate, although quite sufficient to enable you to compose your daily meals. The more often you peruse the following columns the more quickly you'll become aware of what in your kitchen can be used generously and what economically. The table should enable you, moreover, to modify the suggested recipes by replacing one or several of the ingredients with others of the same calorie value.

Milk and Milk Products

Buttermilk, ¼l	45
Condensed milk, un-sweetened (7.5%), 1 tablespoon	22
Condensed milk, un-sweetened (10%), 1 tablespoon	29
Cream (single cream 10%) ⅛l	156
Cream (whipped 28%) ⅛l	378
Full-fat milk (3.3%) ¼l	171
Half-fat milk (1.5%) ¼l (fresh or long life)	128
Yoghurt from skimmed milk, 1 beaker	60
Yoghurt from skimmed milk, with fruit, 1 beaker	100
Skimmed milk, ¼l	46
Soured cream (10%), ⅛l	154

Cheese, per 100g

Blue cheese (50%) fat)	413
Buttercheese (50% fat)	361
Camembert (30% fat)	225
Camembert (40% fat)	297
Camembert (45% fat)	301
Cheddar cheese	430
Cottage cheese	100
Cream cheese (60% fat)	354
Curd cheese, fat-reduced	88
Curd cheese (20% fat)	124
Curd cheese (40% fat)	179
Edam (30% fat)	238
Edam (40% fat)	280
Emmental (45% fat)	417
Gouda (45% fat)	401
Limburg (20% fat)	199

Parmesan (45% fat) grated 1 tablespoon = 10 grams	41
Processed cheese (20% fat)	196
Processed cheese (45% fat)	305
Tilsit (30% fat)	297
Tilsit (45% fat)	374

If cheese is to be used with bread or to gratinate a dish, the best way to proceed is to cut 100g of the cheese in 10 slices of equal size. This will enable you to work out without any difficulty how many calories each individual portion contains.

Eggs

1 egg	84
1 egg yolk	68
1 egg white	16
2 eggs, scrambled or fried with 10g butter	250

Edible fats

Butter, 100g	755
Butter, 1 individual por-tion, 25g	189
Butter, 1 tablespoon, 15g	114
Butter, 1 teaspoon, 5g	38
Hard vegetable fat, 100g	925
Hard vegetable fat, 1 tablespoon, 15g	138

Keeping slim

Hard vegetable fat, 1 teaspoon, 5g	46
Lard, 100g	947
Lard, 1 tablespoon, 15g	142
Lard, 1 teaspoon, 5g	47
Margarine, 100g	733
Margarine, 1 tablespoon, 15g	110
Margarine, 1 teaspoon, 5g	37
Oil, 100g	927
Oil, 1 tablespoon	84
Oil, 1 teaspoon, 3g	28

Bread and Bakery Products

Apple pie	83
Bread roll of 50g	140
1 butter biscuit	20
1 cracker	8
Cheese cake, made from curd cheese, 1 piece	250
Crispbread, 1 slice, 10g	38
1 doughnut	220
Fruit tart on sponge base, 1 slice	200
Graham bread, 1 slice, 40g	100
Jam tart	111
Pumpernickel, 1 slice, 40g	97
Rich fruit cake	104
Rusks, per piece, 10g	40
Rye bread, 1 slice, 40g	101
Starch-reduced toast, 1 slice, 25g	61
Toast, 1 slice	75
Wheat bread, 1 slice, 40g	111
Wholemeal wheat bread, 1 slice, 30g	75
Wholemeal rye bread, 1 slice, 45g	105

Sugar and Sweetmeats

1 chocolate, 15g	80
Cranberry preserve, 1 teaspoon, 10g	27
Honey, 1 teaspoon, 10g	30
Lump sugar, 1 lump 5g	20
Marzipan, 10g	50
Milk chocolate, 100g	563
Milky Way, 1 bar	130
Nougat, 10g	50
Redcurrant jelly, 1 teaspoon, 10g	26
Strawberry jam, 1 teaspoon, 10g (calorie-reduced)	13
Sugar, 100g	394
Sugar, 1 tablespoon, 15g	60
Sugar, 1 teaspoon, 5g	20
Vanilla sugar, 1 packet	39

Pasta and other Farinaceous Foods

Bread crumbs, 1 tablespoon	35
Bread crumbs, 1 teaspoon	12
Corn flakes, 1 tablespoon, 10g	36
Cornflour, 1 tablespoon, 15g	54
Cornflour, 1 teaspoon, 4g	18
Flour, 100g	370
Flour, 1 tablespoon, 10g	37
Flour, 1 teaspoon, 4g	12
Gelatine, 1 leaf, 2g	7
Noodles, uncooked, 50g (1 portion)	180
Porridge oats, 50g	201
Rice, uncooked, 50g (1 portion)	194
Semolina, 1 tablespoon	48

Fish and Crustaceans

1 anchovy	15
1 anchovy fillet, 5g	7
Anchovy paste, 1 teaspoon	21
Anchovy fillet, rolled, in oil, per piece	24
Bass, smoked, 100g	157
Buckling, 1 of 250g	232
Caviar substitute, 100g	135
Cod, 100g	77
Cod, fried	199
Crayfish, shelled, 100g	71
Crayfish, canned, 100g	95
Fish fingers	192
Flounder, 100g	79
Flounder, smoked, 100g	121
Haddock, 100g	80
Haddock, smoked, 100g	102
Herrings in aspic, 100g	176
Herring fillets in tomato sauce, 100g	217
Lobster meat, 100g	89
Mussels, shelled, 100g	72
Oysters, shelled, 100g	71
Perch, 100g	94
Plaice, 100g	83
Pike, 100g	89
Prawns, shelled, 100g	103
Ruff, 100g	112
Salmon, smoked, 100g	108
Salmon trout, 100g	108
Salmon, 100g	88
Sea pike, 100g	84
Shrimps, shelled, 100g	103
Scampi, shelled, 100g	80
Spider lobster, shelled, 100g	82
Sole, 100g	90
Turbot, 100g	89
Trout, 100g	104

Keeping slim

Butcher's Meat (cuts containing relatively few calories; per 100g)

Beef, steak	133
Beef, fillet	126
Beef, brisket	144
Beef, clod	131
Beef, rump	151
Calf's tongue	134
Calf's kidneys	138
Calf's liver	143
Calf's brain	128
Calf's heart	129
Calf's sweetbread	108
Lamb fillet	122
Lamb's heart	169
Lamb's brain	135
Lamb's liver	131
Lamb, escalope	142
Ox heart	133
Ox brain	137
Ox liver	141
Ox kidney	122
Ox tongue	197
Pig's liver	147
Pig's kidneys	125
Pig's tongue	140
Pork cutlets	358
Pork, escalope	168
Veal, breast	142
Veal, fillet	105
Veal, knuckle	107
Veal, cutlets	125
Veal, escalope	108

Meat and Sausage Products (100g)

The following are a selection of the most commonly-consumed sausage products, all rather rich in calories. You're advised once again to cut the 100g you buy into 10 slices, thus giving yourself a good idea of how many calories you consume per slice.

Bacon	476
Beef, minced for tatar	128
Black pudding	425
Bockwurst	294
Cervelat sausage	484
Corned beef	225
Frankfurt sausages	256
Ham, cooked	282
Ham, smoked	395
Jagdwurst	346
Knackwurst	372
Liver sausage	449
Lyons sausage	329
Meat sausage	315
Mettwurst	551
Mortadella	367
Pickled tongue	205
Pork sausage	369
Salami	550
Sausages in cans	239
Steak and kidney pie	304
Vienna sausages	264

Game and Poultry (per 100g)

Chicken, frying	144
Chicken, boiling	274
Chicken breast	109
Chicken heart	137
Chicken liver	147
Chicken drumsticks	120
Duck	243
Goose	364
Hare	124
Partridge	200
Pheasant	111
Pigeon	102
Rabbit meat	167
Turkey	282
Venison	123
Venison, leg	106
Venison, saddle	133

Vegetables (containing relatively few calories; per 100g, unless otherwise stated)

Artichokes	30
1 artichoke, approx. 200g	60
Artichoke bottoms, 1 can of 220g	134
Artichoke hearts, 1 can of 250g	152
1 aubergine 250g	60
Avocado	140
Baked beans	92
Beetroot, pickled	40
Broccoli	20
Brussels sprouts	50
Cabbage	25
Cabbage, boiled	8
Carrots	30
Celeriac	38
Chanterelles	34
Chicory	16
Chinese cabbage	13
Chives, chopped fine, 1 tablespoon	1
Courgettes	11
Corn salad	17

Keeping slim

Cress	28	**Fruit, fresh and canned**		**Spicy Sauces and Appetizers**	
Curly kale	23	(per 100g, unless otherwise			
Cucumber	10	stated)		Barbecue sauce, 1 table-	
Endive salad	16			spoon	15
Fennel, 200g	92	Apple	52	Bismarck herring, 100g	203
French beans	31	1 apple, approximately		Chilli sauce, 1 tablespoon	23
Kohl-rabi	26	80g	40	Cornichon, 1 small	1
Leeks	38	Apple purée, canned	79	Cucumber, sweet-sour,	
Lettuce	15	Apricots, fresh	54	each	20
Mushrooms	24	Apricots, canned	93	Cumberland sauce, 1 table-	
Olives, green	146	1 banana, approximately		spoon	37
Onions	45	150g	108	Dill pickle, each	15
Onions, 1 medium sized	20	Bilberries (blueberries)	60	French dressing, 1 table-	
Parsley, chopped, 1 table-		Bilberries, preserved	101	spoon	62
spoon	1	Blackcurrants	46	Ginger, preserved	340
Pepper	22	Cherries	64	Herb sauce, 2 tablespoons	15
Peas, green, fresh	75	Cherries, canned	80	Horseradish, grated, 1 tea-	
Peas and carrots mixed,		Cranberries	43	spoon, 5g	4
deep-frozen	53	Cranberries, preserved	274	Horseradish sauce, 1 table-	
Potatoes, unpeeled	72	Figs, dried	140	spoon	77
Potatoes, peeled (3 small)	85	Grapes	74	Instant meat broth ¼l	7
Pumpkin	32	Grapefruit (1) about 150g	57	Italian dressing, 1 table-	
Radishes	20	Mandarins	31	spoon	98
Red cabbage	21	Morello cherries	50	Mango chutney, 1 table-	
Sauerkraut	28	Morello cherries, canned	70	spoon	35
Spinach	23	1 orange, peeled	49	Mayonnaise, (50%)	
Sweetcorn	80	Peaches, canned	79	1 tablespoon 33g	150
Tomatoes	10	1 peach, about 150g	65	Mayonnaise (80%)	
Wax beans	27	1 pear, approx. 125g	65	1 tablespoon 33g	225
		Pears, canned	72	Mustard sauce, 1 table-	
		Pineapple, fresh	58	spoon	65
		Pineapple, canned, 1 slice	35	Mustard, 1 teaspoon	4
		Plums	53	Mustard pickles, 1 table-	
		Raspberries	40	spoon	29
		Raspberries, deep-frozen,		Paprika sauce, 2 table-	
		sugared	111	spoons	19
		Redcurrants	38	Pearl onions pickled, each	1
		Rhubarb	16	Remoulade sauce (50%),	
		Strawberries	40	1 tablespoon	150
		Water melon	23	Rollmops, 150g	380
		Yellow plums	63		

Keeping slim

Shashlik sauce, 1 table-spoon	29	
Soya sauce, 1 tablespoon	10	
Tomato ketchup, 1 table-spoon	35	
Tomato purée, 1 table-spoon	15	

Beverages

Apple juice, ¼l	118
Beer, dark, ¼l	120
Beer, light, ¼l	117
Blackcurrant juice, ¼l	130
Bordeaux wine, ¼l	190
Brandy, 2cl	50
Brown ale, ¼l	140
Burgundy wine, ¼l	195
Carrot juice, ¼l	80
Champagne, ¼l	310
Cider, 10dl	42
Clear spirits, 2cl	37
Egg liqueur, 2cl	50
Gin, 10dc	222
Ginger ale, ¼l	70
Grapefruit juice, ¼l	118
Grape juice, black, ¼l	184
Grape juice, white, ¼l	168
Kirsch, 2cl	67
Lemon juice, 1 tablespoon	4
Madeira wine, 15cl	59
Moselle wine, ¼l	160
Orange juice, fresh or deep-frozen ¼l	163
Orange juice, canned, ¼l	130
Port, 5cl	70
Raspberry brandy, 2cl	47
Redcurrant juice, ¼l	125
Red wine, ordinary, ¼l	175
Rum, 2cl	74

Sauerkraut juice, ¼l	17
Sherry, dry, 5cl	58
Soda water	0
Tomato juice, ¼l	50
Vegetable juice, mixed ¼l	70
White wine, ordinary, ¼l	175
Whisky, 4cl	100

Keeping slim

Calorie traps!

Items of food and drink with high-calorie content but without appreciable nutritive value:

Brandy, gin, rum or whisky, 4cl	100
Chocolate, 1 piece	50
Chocolate, plain, 1 piece	26
Chocolate, 100g	563
Cream gateau, 1 piece	500
Doughnuts, each	200
Mayonnaise (80%), 1 tablespoon, 33g	225
Potato crisps, each	10
Potato chips, each	20
Salt stick or Pretzel, 1 piece	20
Stuffed puff pastry tartlets, each	280
Sweet (candy), one piece	40
Sugar, 1 teaspoon, 5g	20
Toast, 1 slice, 30g	75

Items of food with a high-calorie content but of high nutritive value

Almonds, 100g	650
Apricots, dried, 100g	300
Brazil nuts, 100g	714
Dates, dried, 100g	305
Figs, dried, 100g	270
Hazelnuts, 100g	690
Honey, 1 teaspoon, 10g	30
Ice-cream, 100g	205
Peanuts, 100g	630
Plums, dried, 100g	290
Walnuts, 100g	705

Protein table

Foodstuffs particularly rich in proteins
Unless otherwise stated the protein quantities are for 100g.

Almonds	18.3g
Beef, fillet	19.2g
Beef, chuck or buttock	19.4g
Beef, rump	17.4g
Beef, tatar	21.3g
Buckling	21.8g
Calf's liver	19.2g
Chicken breast	22.8g
Chicken meat	20.6g
Chicken liver	22.1g
Crispbread	10.1g
Halibut	18.6g
Haricot beans	21.3g
Hazelnuts	13.9g
Lamb, leg	18 g
Lamb, shoulder	15.6g
Lentils	23.5g
Mackerel	18.8g
Ox liver	19.7g
Parmesan cheese	3.6g
Peanuts	26.5g
Pig's liver	20.6g
Pork fillet	18.6g
Pork escalope	20.8g
Porridge oats	13.8g
Rabbit meat	20.8g
Sole	17.5g
Split peas	22.9g
Trout	19.1g
Turkey	20.1g
Veal, escalope	20.7g
Veal, shoulder	20.9g
Venison (saddle)	20.4g
Walnuts	14.6g
Wholewheat bread	8.4g
Wholemeal bread	7.3g

Index

Index